THE DIGESTED READ

THE DIGESTED READ

JOHN CRACE

RDR Books
Muskegon, Michigan • Berkeley, California

The Digested Read

published in the United States and Canada by:
RDR Books
1487 Glen Avenue
Muskegon, MI 49441
Phone: 510 595-0595
Fax: 510 228-0300
E-mail: Read@rdrbooks.com
Website: www.rdrbooks.com

First published in 2005 by Guardian Books, London

ISBN 1-57143-159-4
After Jan. 1, 2007: 978-1-57143-159-2

Library of Congress Catalog Card Number 2006900596

Cover illustration and design: Joe Berger
Text design: www.carrstudio.co.uk
Additional typograpy (US edition): Richard Harris

Printed in Canada by Transcontinental Printing

Contents

Sport   55

Selective memories   67

Dear diary   108

Thrillers 123

Very serious fiction 139

Sex; sex; sex 175

Help & self-help 185

Americana 209

Lad lit 229

Introduction

It's normal for an author to use an introduction to thank their publisher and agent. It helps spread the blame if things go pear-shaped, and appears generous if, by a slim chance, the book sells. I would like to break with tradition by extending my thanks to everyone else's agents and publishers. Without them, there would be no Digested Read.

No one can quite remember whose idea the Digested Read first was, but I am delighted to have inherited it more than five years ago. The idea of rewriting a book in the style of the author in just 500 or so words is a gift to any satirist, and it remains the only outlet in the print media where publishers' hype always gets treated with the irreverence it deserves.

The basic premise for the Digested Read is that it should be the book that has created the most media noise that week. Many books simply choose themselves – you can't ignore the new Martin Amis, however much you might want to. I aim to be catholic in my choices – non-fiction and mass-market titles are always up for grabs – but I veer towards the literary fiction heavyweights, because these are the books that often generate the most column inches.

Publishing is an industry like any other and books are published on their perceived ability to make money. Literary merit is often merely an added bonus. It goes without saying that authors with big reputations tend to sell more, even though their books often fail to match their reputation.

It's in no one's interest to tell our finest authors that something isn't working or that 100 pages could safely be cut without anyone noticing. Schedules would be disrupted, departments would miss budget, the company share price would fall and, to make matters even worse, the authors might take their next books to a different publishing house. All in all, everyone would be very pissed off indeed. Far better to keep quiet, roll out a high-profile PR and marketing campaign and wait for the money to roll in.

You can't even trust the reviews to find out whether a book will be worth the £16.99 price tag. The literary world is very, very small and a lot of back scratching goes on as almost everybody knows everybody else. It's only the readers who are kept out of the loop.

At least with the Digested Read you know where you are. I won't have been having lunch with Salman Rushdie. Or his agent. Or his publisher. You could argue that I read the books slightly differently to everyone else because my antennae are honed towards clunky plot devices that don't work, pretentious stylistic tics, and a complete absence of ideas. But I have to invent almost nothing. The author does the work for me.

Occasionally I can do nice. Very occasionally. In the time I've been writing the Digested Read, only a couple have been so flawless that they have resisted the knife. I'll leave you to work out which they are. In the meantime, writers, agents and publishers: please keep those books coming. Your business is my business.

Prizewinners

True History of the Kelly Gang

Peter Carey

My da were put in prison by the traps for a crime he didn't do and I know that to be true as it were me that stole the heifer but we were poor and hungry and what else were I to do. That last time inside broke him truly it did and he died soon after and my blessed mother got some land 60 crabholed miles north and it were I who tried to look after it as I were now the oldest man even though I were only 12.

Uncle James soon came round to deliver his attentions to me ma and they werent wanted I can tell you so I kicked him in the bawbles to get him off. He were effing and shouting adjectival this and adjectival that and he then set fire to the home before the traps came and took him away but neither me ma or me would say a word against him at the assizes. Harry Power the bushranger came round to see me ma too and I became his apprentice; he bought me a pair of boots and he made me help him hold up a coach but I didnt think this were right when I seen him rob some poor people sos I escaped. What are you doing said me ma with her arms around Bill Frost; I paid 15 quid to have Harry takes you.

Harry threatened to kill Bill Frost when he said he wouldn't pay to keep my mother and I set off a musket by accident and at that point Harry and I were one again people said I were criminal but I were just gullible seeing as I was only just 16. I were taken by the traps over a stolen horse and the lying adjectival says I has betrayed Harry when he were caught but I were no fizgig or dobber as me mother knew.

Mary Hearn were as good a woman as ever lived and she gave me you but Constable Fitzpatrick were a cur for what he done to my sister and we treated him right considering; but the traps they hunted us down to Stringybark Creek and I promise you that all the killings that were done were all in self-defence.

The Euroa Bank robbery were not the way it were written in the paper but we was getting famous now. I would not of wanted Aaron to die even though he was a traitor but Joe insisted and the traps they soon surrounded us at the Glenrowan hotel and I made some armour and walked out firing.

The digested read ... digested

Australias notorious outlaw finds a voice and tries to put the record straight truly he does.

Youth

JM Coetzee

He lives in a one-room flat near Mowbray railway station for which he pays 11 guineas a month. He is at pains not to be late with the rent because he has obtained the flat under false pretences. He has given his occupation as library assistant rather than student. It is not quite a lie as he does man the reading room every weekday evening. Every Sunday he boils up marrowbones to make enough soup to last a week. He is proving man is an island.

He has a best friend, Paul, also a mathematician, who is having an affair with an older woman named Elinor. Her sister, Jacqueline, takes him for a walk on the beach. He does not resist and goes through with the act. He knows that she will not have enjoyed their lovemaking either, but he knows enough to say nothing. Within a week she has moved in with him. He finds her presence claustrophobic. She finds his diary. She leaves.

He is reading the Cantos of Ezra Pound and dreams of being a poet. He gets a girl named Sarah pregnant. They fail to connect. She has an abortion. They separate. After Sharpeville, he senses revolution in the air. He moves to London.

He gets a job as a computer programmer with IBM and each morning he dons his dark suit, waiting for the weekend when he can see a Bergman film or go to the Reading Room. He joins a poetry group and meets a woman. They get undressed but there is no warmth between them. They say "sorry" to one another and part. He thinks perhaps he is homosexual. He picks up a man. They say nothing. Is this homosexuality?

He is turned down for a flatshare. He is too boring. His misery is almost complete. His mother writes to him every week, but he replies only rarely. To do otherwise would smack of reciprocation. He meets a Swedish girl named Astrid. They go to bed, but he feels discomforted by her proximity. He pretends to sleep when she lets herself out.

He leaves IBM and attempts to write like Henry James. He fails. He joins International Computers and feels he's sold his soul to the Americans. He reads Beckett. He meets an Indian programmer named Ganapathy and invites him for a meal but he does not turn up. He reflects on his life. He has failed as both a lover and a writer. He sits alone.

The digested read ... digested

Coetzee goes for triple Booker win with early-60s existential ennui.

The Line of Beauty

Alan Hollinghurst

1983

"I'm the only gay in the £1m Kensington town house," shrieked Nick.

"Well, I'm the only manic-depressive," declared Cat.

"Oh, what a languid torpor descends upon us all," said Tobias. "I wonder what job pater will find for me."

Nick retired to his room. How different it all was from his own suburban upbringing. A few bars of Schumann played in his head as he thought of Tobias's sensual body. "Stop it," he told himself. He and Tobias had been friends – just friends – since Oxford and now he was an adoptive member of the Fedden family.

"Hello, everyone," said Gerald, the Tory MP who was Tobias and Cat's father. "And isn't Margaret just the Lady?"

"Gosh yes," smarmed Nick and Tobias.

Nick snuck out to see his working-class lover.

"Neither I nor my ex are at all well," whispered Leo.

"Never mind," Nick whispered. Then they had sex.

It was the evening of the grandest party of the year.

"I'm a lady," said Lady Partridge.

"I'm a lady, too," Nick smiled, high on excitement. His bedroom had a Louis XV *escritoire*, and anyone who was anyone was there.

1986

Nick and Wani snorted cocaine, and then Nick watched as Wani was sodomised by a rent boy.

"Here," laughed Wani. "Have £5,000."

Nick placed the cheque in his designer trousers. A chord played in his head. He hoped it was from Wagner. He longed to tell the world he and Wani were lovers, but Wani insisted on secrecy.

"What is it you and Wani are doing?" Gerald asked.

"We're producing a style magazine," Nick said.

"Top hole," Gerald replied. "Why don't you come to our chateau? I'm desperate to spend my oodles of cash."

"Really," said Cat, as she and Nick lazed by the pool, "fancy you and Wani being an item. I'm sure pater's fucking my boyfriend."

It was the evening of the grandest party of the year.

"Have you heard?" said Cat. "Leo's died of Aids."

"I'm going to dance with Margaret," Nick flounced.

1987

Wani was dying of Aids.

"It's what happens to common people whose family made their fortune in retail," muttered Cat to Nick.

"I've been told that pater's about to be exposed for insider dealing," said Tobias.

"And that's not all," Cat gasped. "He's also been fucking his secretary. I'm going to expose his Tory hypocrisy to the papers."

"You are not really one of us," said Gerald to Nick. "You've bought ruin on this family and you must leave."

As Nick walked through Notting Hill, he knew his test result would be positive.

The digested read ... digested

Little Britain meets Evelyn Waugh.

Never Let Me Go

Kazuo Ishiguro

My name is Kathy H. I am a carer. As I drive around the country looking after my donors, I like to reflect, in my elegant and refined way, on my childhood at Hailsham.

I realise now how lucky Tommy, Ruth and I were to be brought up in such surroundings. We even had a sports pavilion where we would go to chatter amongst ourselves. You may wonder why I mention these details, but such empty observations are the hallmark of the consummate prose stylist.

From time to time, we would talk about donations and the world outside, and then we would shrink back into our sheltered lives. It may strike you that I like to hint at truths. This is because I fear you might stop reading were you to guess that the story really was as predictable as it first seemed.

Our guardians, particularly Miss Emily, took good care of us. Most of us, apart from poor Tommy, became competent artists and we were, in our way, quite happy, though a sense of dread would run through the school when Madame came by to take the pick of our artwork.

We had very few personal possessions but that never bothered us. My treasured item was a Julie Bridgewater tape. How I loved to dance to it! Sadly, it got lost one day.

I can see you are becoming deeply affected by the poignancy of our situation. I should have loved to have told you at this point of how we felt about having no parents, of how we tried to escape into the outside world. But I can't. Emotion and interest have no part in this story.

As we grew older we started to have sex with one another, though the enjoyment was tempered by the fact that none of us could have children. Tommy and Ruth even became a couple when the three of us left Hailsham and went to live at The Cottages.

Improbable as it may seem, I used to enjoy looking at porn mags, though this was partly because I hoped to spot my possible. We were all obsessed with meeting our possibles – our real-world entities – and Ruth once thought she had seen hers in Norwich. But it turned out to look nothing like her, which left her depressed for days. I suspect you're beginning to know how she felt.

Ruth and Tommy split up before Ruth made her first donation and she completed while making her second. I became Tommy's carer and we started to have sex after his third donation. We hoped to defer his fourth donation for a few years, but a chance meeting with Madame and Miss Emily stopped that.

"Deferrals are not possible," Miss Emily said. "You are mere clones – organ donors – and we've tried to make you as happy as possible."

This came as quite a shock, though I dare say not to you. Tommy completed during his fourth donation so I'm left alone, to drone on.

The digested read ... digested

The triumph of style over substance.

Life of Pi

Yann Martel

My name came from a swimming pool. Piscine Molitor Patel. At my first school, the other boys called me Pissing, so when I moved I changed my name to Pi. I've spent a lot of my life looking for God. That's why I'm a Hindu, Muslim and a Christian. I'm not sure why I've never converted to Judaism or Shinto. My father ran the zoo in Pondicherry. He really loved his animals, so when the zoo had to close he decided to bring them with us to Canada.

The Tsimstum sank several days out of harbour. My father, mother and brother all drowned. I had been taking a walk on the deck when the ship went down and was thrown into the lifeboat by a couple of sailors. I came to and found myself sharing a boat with a zebra with a broken leg and a hyena. Shortly afterwards, I made the mistake of helping Richard Parker aboard. Richard Parker was a Bengal tiger.

The hyena started eating the zebra alive. The zebra howled piteously. Richard Parker just looked on. An orang-utan floated by on a huge mound of bananas. The hyena had him as well.

As we all got hungrier I became more anxious. Before long the hyena and Richard Parker were locked in battle. Richard Parker won, and the pair of us began our strange life aboard.

I learned how to provide him with fresh drinking water, and shared the flying fish I caught. I had to work hard to make him accept I was the alpha male. As the weeks turned into months, our food began to run out and we went blind. "How are you?" said Richard Parker. Fancy Richard Parker being able to speak, I thought. But it wasn't Richard Parker. It was a blind Frenchman in the middle of the Pacific. Richard Parker ate him, too.

Later we made landfall. It was no ordinary landfall, as it was just a floating mass of algae and trees. Richard Parker ate the meerkats. We left when we discovered the island was carnivorous.

After 277 days at sea, we reached Mexico. Richard Parker made a dash for the jungle. I was picked up and looked after by the locals. Two Japanese officials from the shipping company came to find out what happened. I told them, but they didn't believe me.

"Would you prefer if I said my family escaped with me, but died on the way?"

"That's much better," they said.

The digested read ... digested

Johnny Morris goes to sea and returns with the Booker. Or did I dream that last bit?

Saturday

Ian McEwan

Henry Perowne wakes early in a state of near euphoria. He gets up quietly in order not to disturb his wife, Rosalind, who lies sleeping. Like the neurosurgeon he is, he clinically dissects his mood. Has he perhaps become a little too smug and self-satisfied? No, he deserves to be extremely rich and happy.

"Hello birds, hello trees," he says to himself before he notices an arc of flame cross the sky. He watches as an aeroplane with engines ablaze struggles over his Bloomsbury house, and waits for the explosion that never comes. He is unsettled, wondering if this presages a terrorist attack. How quickly one's life can alter, he thinks, and how curious not to know for sure.

He tiptoes downstairs where his son Theo is drinking a cup of tea. Perowne is as proud of Theo, who is already at just 18 one of the world's leading blues guitarists, as he is of his daughter Daisy, the foremost young poet of her generation, who is returning home from Paris this evening for the first time in six months. He switches on the news to find there was no terrorist incident and that the plane has landed safely. What strange tricks the mind can play, he thinks.

Henry returns upstairs. Rosalind welcomes him and they make love passionately. He loves her now as much as the day his dexterity saved her from blindness more than 20 years ago. "I love you only," he whispers. "I adore you, too," she replies.

He drives towards his weekly squash match with Strauss. The streets are blocked because of the anti-war march. Henry can see the case both for and against the invasion of Iraq. How complicated life can be, he thinks, when you think so deeply and so philosophically and are yet so happy. A car brushes past him and breaks off his wing mirror. Three men get out and threaten him. One, Baxter, hits him in the chest. Perowne looks him in the eye and diagnoses Huntington's disease. The news confuses Baxter, who backs off.

Bugger, thinks Perowne, upset at having lost to Strauss, as he drives back from his mother's. He should be more disturbed by her Alzheimer's but he's concentrating on his happiness.

The evening is not devoid of tension. Daisy is withholding something and Rosalind's father is drunk, but the mood is mellowing when Baxter breaks in and threatens them with a knife. He orders Daisy to get undressed and Henry observes she is pregnant. Theo tenses his heroic muscular physique and pushes Baxter to the ground.

Henry must perform emergency surgery on Baxter. He harvests two long strips of pericranium and repairs the tear in the dura. He flicks his gloves. Whatever Baxter may have done, he was owed another chance.

He and Rosalind fall into each others arms. "Everything's going to be happy," he says. And now the day is over.

The digested read ... digested

McNasty serves up a McHappy Meal.

Vernon God Little

DBC Pierre

It's hot as fucken hell in Martirio, the barbecue-sauce capital of central Texas. I'm sitting on the porch when Deputy Vaine Gurie knocks on the door.

"Vernon Gregory Little," she says. "I'm arresting you for conspiracy to murder 14 of your classmates."

"I didn't fucken do nothing," I grunt.

"I believe you," screams my mom. "Oh my God, my son's a fucken serial killer."

Trouble fucken rocks when you're just 15. So my Mescan mate Jesus Navarro took out half the class and blew his fucken brains out, and they need a fall guy who's alive. Too bad most of my witnesses are dead, and they'll never find the place I had a shit that proves I wasn't fucken there.

The judge has given me bail, but my mom's just freakin out. "I'm gonna be famous and on TV," she says. "Lally from CNN has asked me to give him some money to make a film about life as a killer's mom in murder city."

"He's not from CNN and I'm innocent."

"Sure, killer," she smiles.

I've gotta get rid of the fucken spliffs I've been holding for Taylor Figueroa. Christ, she was so stoned I coulda got my hands inside her panties, but like the fucken dumbass I am, I went and got her friends. Maybe she could still fall in love with a fugitive.

Mom has fucken given all my lawnmowin money to Lally. How the fuck am I gonna get to Mexico? Me and Ella scam some cash out of that old perve Mr Deutschmann and I'm off.

I call Taylor. "Hi, killer," she says. "Do you wanna borrow $600?" I go to the Acapulco Western Union. "Surprise," she goes. She takes me back to her hotel and peels off her shorts. "Tell me you killed them for me." What the hell. "I did it for you."

"I got it on tape," she shouts, pullin up her shorts. "I'm gonna be famous."

"Nice work," grins Lally.

Back in Martirio the death count is rising and I'm being blamed for the lot. I get not guilties on all except the fucken high school massacre. So now I'm waitin on fucken death row, with a web cam following my every move. The town has become the country's murder capital, the media are everywhere, and everyone's become a millionaire except for me.

"We found the shit," someone yells. "You're pardoned."

The digested read ... digested

Innocent boy escapes the death penalty in Texas. Yup, it's fiction.

Fury

Salman Rushdie

Professor Malik Solanka, retired historian of ideas, internationally renowned doll-maker, and still powerfully attractive in his fifty-sixth year, gazed down from his New York apartment. His Fury rose – how he despised the pre-synaptic materialism of the gnomic ants below.

The phone rang. It was his wife Eleanor. What could he say? That she hadn't given him enough blow jobs? Surely not that he'd quit their marriage after finding himself bathed in Fury, knife in hand, poised to kill both her and their son Asmaan and had needed to put 3,000 miles between them.

Money, at least, wasn't a problem. Colleagues had sneered when he'd renounced academia in favour of doll-making and had openly laughed when his series, Little Brain, featuring a woman interrogating the great philosopher, had first been broadcast. But, he, Malik, had shown them, and several series, books and franchise toys later, the laugh was on them.

The papers were full of the Concrete Killer, the slayer of three New York society beauties. Could he have done it, Malik wondered. His drinking was affecting his memory.

"Are you the creator of Little Brain?" asked Mila, empress of the street.

He acknowledged he was. "I love them," she continued.

"I hate them," he replied. "They fill me with Fury."

"Come, lie down next to me," she cooed.

Malik felt uncomfortable and wondered if he was a father substitute.

"Neela's left me," said Jack to Malik.

"I need to speak," said Neela to Malik.

Several men walked into lamp posts, so overwhelmed were they by Neela's beauty. Malik and Neela kissed deeply. He was old enough to be her father, but this was clearly true love.

"Jack's dead," Neela said a week later. "He was killed by the boyfriends of the three society beauties who all turned out to be the Concrete Killer. Now please help me save my little island of Lilliput-Blefuscu."

"I'd love to, once I've finished my new series of dolls," he cooed.

"Who do you think you are?" Malik awoke to find Mila and Eleanor shouting at him, while Neela quietly dressed.

The following week, Malik flew to Lilliput-Blefuscu to find Neela. "You're a lucky man," said one of the hostages. "Neela sacrificed her life in the coup, but her last act was to save yours."

The digested read ... digested

Self-regarding fiftysomething man dumps his wife, moves to New York, meets the most beautiful woman in the world and writes about it.

Porno

Irvine Welsh

The phone goes an it's me aunt Paula sayin: "Why don't you come an run the Port Sunshine in Leith?" I've had enough of this shit-arse stretch of Soho, so's I send Begbie a load of gay porno in the nick an I'm on the train up north.

* * *

Rab takes me down the pub and we meet Juice Terry who's making stag films. "I could do that," I say. "You aren't half shaggable, Nikki," he answers.

* * *

I'm back in my hometown. Simon Williamson. No more Sick Boy. I'm done with all that shite. Just the odd few lines of ching to keep me goin. I bumps into Juice Terry, who knows people in the Dam an I says we should do some proper porno together.

* * *

Ma heid's buzzin but ah'm crackin oan noo ah'm oot. Goat to git pished n ah'm gaunnae find the fuckin cunt that was sendin ays the poof's porn thin ah'm goan look for that fuckin cunt Rent Boy.

* * *

I'm mindin me own business in the Dam when fuckin Sick Boy comes in shouting, "Where's my fuckin money, Rent Boy, you cunt?" Then he nuts me an asks me to join his scam.

* * *

"Beautiful, Nikki," says Simon as I give him the bank numbers I've scammed off the nerd. "I think I love you," I reply. "You're goin to be a star," he says. "I won't do anal, though," I goes.

* * *

32

£64,000 in the bank an a film in the can. Nikki was pissed off that I cut the film to make it look like she's done anal, but she was well pleased we're off to Cannes.

* * *

Ah fuckin doan in Chizzie bot noans grassin ays up. Whaires that Rent Boy?

* * *

Fuck Cannes. Fuck Sick Boy. I've emptied the fuckin bank account an all I got to do is avoid Begbie.

* * *

I'm all chinged up, I've come all over Nikki and fuckin Rent Boy's done me again. I phones Begbie. "Rent Boy's in town, do him."

* * *

I sees Begbie comin for me an he's knocked down by a fuckin car.

* * *

I looks down at Begbie. "I've lost me money an you're fuckin fucked, you cunt," I says. "You're good as deid." His eyes open and his hand grabs me throat.

The digested read ... digested

Sick Boy, Rent Boy and Begbie line up for a return heid to heid.

Short stories

To Cut a Long Story Short

Jeffrey Archer

The master storyteller slid his Mont Blanc fountain pen into the inside pocket of his Savile Row suit and sighed. "Where did it all go wrong?" he said to himself, as he got up from his hand-tooled leather armchair and paced over to the panoramic windows of his penthouse which commanded the finest views in the whole of London.

As he stretched lazily, his gold cufflinks, engraved with the famous Grantchester crest which had been bestowed on his family in recognition of years of tireless public service, glinted in the late-afternoon sunlight and drew his attention to the the giant Millennium Wheel that dominated the London skyline. "Damn it," he muttered. "I once had a vision for this city, too."

But Jeffrey was not a man to dwell on the negative: after all, he still had a contract to write a book of short stories. "I'll show them all what they're missing," he mouthed grimly. His mind drifted back to happier days, and a kernel of an idea emerged. "I had a wonderful time at Oxford University," he mused, "but just imagine if I hadn't been there at all. A court case that collapsed because the expert witness's qualifications didn't stand up to scrutiny would be a neat twist." That was the first story taken care of.

The master storyteller was on a roll. All he needed was a series of dramatic life events that had never happened to him and he had his latest collection in the bag. Within hours he had knocked out a second tale about a very rich man who only pretended to have lost all his money. How he chortled at that one.

Succulent aromas wafting in from the kitchen disturbed his creativity and reminded Jeffrey of the fragrant Mary, the bedrock of his life. How could any man do anything to hurt such a woman? But just suppose there was such a man ... a man who liked his mistress to dress as a whore while they had sex in an NCP car park in Mayfair. Story three was in the bag.

Within a week the book was finished. There was the story of the publishing scam based on the price of an advert in a brochure for a Conservative party fundraiser; there was the smug, untalented artist who lived off the generosity of his hard-working family; there was the legal financial con; there was the man who ruined his career on a sexual impulse; there was the man who fell for a get-rich-quick scheme; and, finally, there was the high-powered businessman who was about to be forced to resign from his job and secretly hankered after the simplicity of a tramp.

"Hmm," said Jeffrey, admiring the neatness of his joined-up writing on the final manuscript. Making up stories really isn't very difficult at all.

The digested read ... digested

Deluded self-publicist unwittingly pioneers new literary genre by writing his autobiography as a collection of fictional short stories.

The Lemon Table

Julian Barnes

Julian looked at himself in the mirror with distaste. His face felt saggy and tufts of stray hair sprouted from his nose and ears. Growing old was an insult to the gods. He remembered the very first time he had gone to the barber's on his own as a child. How frightening, yet how grown up it had seemed. Now he might as well be invisible as the stylist went about her business.

He closed the door and walked to the day room. Oh God. There was that dull Swede who went on and on about some unconsummated 40-year love affair between Anders Boden and Mrs Lindwall. It was obviously meant to be a lyrical reflection on the beauty and sadness of the unexpressed, but it was just plain boring. Maybe it was just the way he told it, he thought in a moment of compassion. After all, old people do tend to repeat themselves.

Ah, there was Babs. "I bet she was a looker in her day," he muttered to himself. Not that he could do that much about it. He used to be able to fuck three times a day; now he'd be lucky to do it even once. He was reminded of the anecdote about the retired sergeant major who had visited the same prostitute each year at the regiment dinner. The last time he went, he found out she had died.

Julian sank back into a reverie as Merrill and Janice wittered on about their wonderful, adoring, long-dead husbands. He felt like shouting "Shut the fuck up" because everyone in the nursing home knew that one husband had been gay and the other a serial adulterer. But what was the point? It kept them happy, he supposed.

"Story time," shouted the care worker. Julian groaned. Not another third-rate offering from Granta's latest list of Young British Novelists. "I was on that list once," he spluttered. "Of course you were, dear." Julian ignored her: "Writers today haven't even read Tolstoy, Turgenev or Flaubert, let alone dined with them."

He marched over to the gramophone, placed a 78 of Mozart K595 on the platter. Various old crones started hawking into their spittoons. "Don't any of you know how to behave in the concert hall?" he yelled. "Fuck off," retorted Mart, the youngest care home resident.

Julian sloped off to his bedroom. He looked inside his bedside table for his fan letters. It might have been 20 years ago, and the fan had been rather elderly, but Mrs Winstanley had been a nice old bird. Shame she'd died.

Time for lunch. It was torture watching food being traduced in this way, but there was little he could do. Still, he might be able to get his own back on Mart by tripping him up in the dinner queue. And then it would be back to his writing. Everyone was waiting for his latest opus, but old age did slow the creative process. It was so hard to get continuity when you needed a nap.

"Wake up, Mr Barnes," said the nurse. "It's time for your medication."

The digested read ... digested

I simply don't believe it.

Small Crimes in an Age of Abundance

Matthew Kneale

As they left the station, Guy and Chloe secretly admitted to one another that China was scarier than they had expected. And it hadn't helped that they had mispronounced Guangfaochu and had arrived in the wrong town.

"Someone's stolen all my jewels," Chloe exclaimed.

"It must have been that interpreter," Guy decided. "I'm going to report him."

"There is no crime in this town," the police insisted. But Guy was adamant and at last an officer said he would deal with it.

"Oh look, my jewels were under the bed the whole time," Chloe shrieked.

"Well, we can't tell the police after that fuss," said Guy.

As they left the hotel, Guy and Chloe saw the interpreter's body in a van.

A bead of sweat formed on Matthew's brow. His last book had won the Whitbread prize and his publishers were demanding a follow-up. But every time he tried he started writing one of Roald Dahl's Tales of the Unexpected. "Dammit," he thought. "I'd better have another go."

Peter and Harriet lived a dull life and all their neighbours were richer than they were. One day Peter found a large bag full of cocaine under a bench in a street. "Even though I'm a solicitor, I'm going to become a drug dealer," he said. Harriet thought this was a good idea and over the next few months they made lots of money. One day they delivered some drugs to a house where their children were staying. Then he was arrested. Peter came to quite like jail.

"It's no good. I just can't stop being Roald," thought Matthew. "Maybe if I put something like **Meanwhile several thousands of miles away** at the end of the story it will sound as if it's connected to the next one."

All the farms near Julio's house were destroyed by the gringo crop-sprayers. Except the one that grew coca plants. "Gringos have stolen everything from us," said Julio's dad, as his family moved to a new home in the mountains. "Surprise, surprise," said grandad, pulling a couple of coca plants from his case. "We'll start afresh."

Time was closing in and Matthew surrendered to his muse, hoping everyone would think his stories of international misunderstandings had coherence and depth. There was the fat American who married a beautiful Chinese peasant, the missionaries who gave a dying girl an aspirin, the posh woman who admired the simplicity of her au pair's life, the Welsh bloke who was estranged from his mates because he had to fight in Iraq, and the family who fell apart and then got back together when a relative died.

One to go. How about a suicide bomber who blows himself up alone as a useless gesture? Matthew pressed the button. And as the manuscript disappeared to his publisher, he saw a naked woman dancing in flames.

The digested read ... digested

Deathly Dahl.

Too Beautiful for You

Rod Liddle

Liddy Lidbourne picked up the phone and called his agent. "Y'know, I'm really hot now, man," he drawled. "It's time I wrote a book."

"What did you have in mind? The inside story of the Today programme?"

"Nah. Like fuck that shit. My new brand is sex, drugs and rock'n'roll. I'm gonna write this story of like this fat, disillusioned chick who's sitting in the office waiting for someone to fix the window. Elsewhere in the building there's this middle-aged bloke who has, like, just been dumped by his mistress. He thinks about committing suicide, but doesn't really want to, and wanders into the fat chick's office hoping for sympathy. She thinks he's come to mend the window and says, 'There it is. Get on with it.' So he fucking jumps." Liddy started cackling.

"Whadya think?"

"It's a start," replied the agent cautiously.

Liddy twiddled his tousled hair, stared at his screen and hammered at the keyboard. "Finished," he yelled half an hour later.

"That's rather quick," the agent said, suspiciously.

"Must be the drugs," smirked Liddy. "Anyway I've knocked out two more stories. There's this one about a girl who gives a bloke a wank rather than shag him, and the other's about a bloke who gets a blow job from his mother-in-law while his wife's buying an ice cream."

"I thought you weren't writing your autobiography," said the agent.

Liddy returned to his office and by the end of the weekend he had cranked out another 200 pages.

"There's some great shit here," he said. "A bloke who's having an affair and tells his wife he's going to Uttoxeter. And, get this, he's, like, in a train crash and gets his arm ripped off and tries to walk to Uttoxeter.

"Yeah, and then there's the bloke who tries to shag the midwife while his wife's giving birth and whose baby can recite the whole Chelsea team. And then there's these two flies that can talk and this posh bird, whose best friend is turning into a locust, who fucks a Romanian tramp. Her mum, like, lives in a teepee and then the Romanian turns out to be a war criminal."

"Do you think you've lost the plot?" said his agent, who was by now extremely concerned for Liddy.

"How can you when there isn't one? I've got another story about a schoolkid who kills loads of people and only gets into trouble when he calls some cunt a nigger, and then there's this Arab who becomes a celebrity for being the world's worst terrorist after failing to detonate his suicide bomb, and then ends up on Parky trying to blow himself up again ..."

Liddy paused. "It's like iconoclastic, man. It's Mart meets Will. I'm the new *enfant terrible*."

His agent shook his head. "Just terrible will do."

The digested read ... digested

The emperor's new clothes unveiled.

(Self)
obsessions

How to Be a (Bad) Birdwatcher

Simon Barnes

Look, up there. In the tree. It's a bird. That makes you a birdwatcher. You may be a bad birdwatcher, but you are still watching birds. I know you don't think you know anything about birds, but I promise you do. You know what a robin and a pigeon look like, don't you? That's all you need to become a birdwatcher. Apart from an ability to count and make lists.

Birdwatching is not at all like trainspotting. That's an activity for dull geeks. Birdwatching is for very exciting geeks who like clamping a pair of binoculars to their forehead for hours on end on the off chance a dodo will come back from the dead. Birds are alive. Now I know dogs are alive, too, but dogwatching isn't much fun.

I first became interested in birdwatching as a child, as I used to spend all my holidays on Streatham Common seeing how many types of warblers I could spot. My dad was high up in the BBC and used to lecture me on the difference between bird sounds. I know more than he does now, and that makes me feel very liberated and grown up.

The great thing about birdwatching is that you do it outdoors, except when you are looking at all the different varieties of tits hovering around the nutfeeder from the kitchen window. I bet you can't tell the difference between all the tits. I can. There's big ones and little ones and blue ones and they all have slightly different habitats. That's interesting.

Birdwatching is nature in the raw. You can be walking along the pavement when – whoomph – a starling flies overhead. You look up and your day is transformed. Suddenly you are overwhelmed by a freedom of the spirit. You don't feel the same when you see a dead hedgehog in the road. That's why poets never write about them. But there are loads of poems about birds.

Sometimes, you might meet other people when you are out birdwatching. But don't worry. You don't have to have any interaction with them, but it can be nice to have a conversation. "Is that a great crested grebe?" is always a good ice-breaker. I once chatted with a girl in Sri Lanka about the rarity of the avocet; we're still married.

There's no need to have a good pair of binoculars – or bins – but they are useful. Only the other day – thanks to my bins – I was able to point out the speculum on the female gadwall to my father. He was very grateful.

Twitchers are not the same as birdwatchers. Twitchers go all over the world and make lists competitively. I've seen loads of birds all over the world and have the lists to prove it. But I'm not competitive, so I'm not a twitcher.

Rejoice in the beauty of birds. Remember. The most revolutionary act is to join the RSPB.

The digested read ... digested

Geekus journalisticus (m): grey plumage, usually bearded, spotted in bookshops around Christmas cashing in on his hobby.

One Hit Wonderland

Tony Hawks

People often say to me, "Tony, is there anything you wouldn't do for a bet?" And I always reply, "It depends whether I can squeeze another book out of it."

Anyway, I'd been chatting to my good friend Arthur – that's Arthur Smith, the famous comedian – about what I should do next, when, blow me, my good friend Jakko, the former guitarist with Level 42, invites me to dinner. There's this gorgeous girl Victoria there, and I just happen to mention I once had a top five hit and appeared on *Top of the Pops* with the single "Stutter Rap". And she yawns, "I bet you can't have another top 20 hit within the next two years."

So here I am in Nashville with my terribly funny country and western song, "You Broke My Heart Like a Bird's Egg, but Now the Yolk's on Me", trying to make a big impression. Actually I'm not, because I know perfectly well no one will take such an idiotic song seriously, but I can't pass up the opportunity to meet some more of my famous chums and get in a few cheap gags at the Yanks' expense.

I may be self-deprecating, but I'd like you to realise I'm seriously talented with it. Got that? Being so famous I get invited on some very important charity gigs. So here I am in Sudan with Unicef with Irvine Welsh and while I'm here I thought I should record some local singers to see if I can mix them into a club hit. Not surprisingly, I can't. Even though I know Simon Cowell from *Pop Idol*.

Bucharest sounded exotic so I thought I'd try to make it big there, too but all that happened was that I was able to use my amazing contacts to get this Romanian singer called Paula a gig duetting with me on the *Gloria Hunniford Show.*

Back on one of my many appearances on Radio 4 panel games, I bumped into Sir Tim Rice. "Sir Tim," I grovelled, "why don't you and I write a hit for me and Norman Wisdom to release in Albania?"

The jolly Albanians were very pleased to see us when we three very important people arrived in Tirana. Anyway Norman and I mimed the song for the TV show and along came the producer to tell us we'd reached No 18 without even releasing a record.

"I've won the bet. I've won the bet," I squealed down the phone to Victoria.

"Zzzzzzzzz," she answered.

The digested read ... digested

Talkative Tony name-drops his way to mediocrity.

31 Songs

Nick Hornby

The conservatory door slammed: Mary was dressed, waiting. Roy Orbison was playing on the radio of my dad's Rover. I gunned the car along the mean streets of Maidenhead and out on to the A4094 towards Beaconsfield. "Live on the edge with Everybloke," I said.

In that moment, Bruce Springsteen spoke to me and I must have played "Thunder Road" 1,500 times – yeah, once a week for 30 years sounds about right. Bruce's songs are all about finding a voice and having one's huge talent recognised. He and I have a lot in common.

So we were doing this charity thing for my son's school and I was a bit nervous, but then I heard Teenage Fanclub playing and I just knew everything would be perfect. Like you do.

And when I started this collection of essays – why 31? Why not? – I assumed every song would be full of time and place connections, but I realised this isn't so because good songs transcend the particular. Which must mean that most of these songs aren't very good because they nearly all relate to specific times in my life.

There again, if you buy a book by me, prose stylist that I am, you want to read about me, don't you? So here are the soundtracks to my son's autism and the break-up of my marriage.

I really hate to let people down – it's a thing with me – and one song that never disappoints is Nelly Furtado's "I'm Like a Bird". I can't even say why it's so good, but it produces in me a narcotic need to hear it again and again. Dave Eggers has a theory that we play songs over and over to solve them; others reckon we're emotionally stunted.

When I first heard Santana's "Samba Pa Ti" I thought it would be the music to which I lost my virginity. In fact this honour fell to Rod Stewart's "Mama, You Been on My Mind". It's always seemed to me that those of us who have stuck with pop music are those that entrusted themselves at a tender age to singers like Stewart. How else could you survive with an imagination that is limited to making lists?

My mum used to complain about the emptiness of pop lyrics but how often do they repeat "Hallelujah" in the *Messiah*?

Classical music and me have never got on and the only reservations I would have about Van Morrison's "Caravan" being played at my funeral is that people might hear the string section and think I'd sold out and become less dull and narrow-minded.

One of the biggest lessons I ever learned in life was that you can walk out. I remember the freedom I experienced when I went to the pub for the drum solo during a Led Zeppelin concert at Earl's Court back in the 70s. So now don't expect me to hang around if something's no good; I might even leave in mid

The digested read ... digested

31 compelling reasons not to make lists.

Lost for Words

John Humphrys

I hate sloppy, overblown, cliche-ridden language when it is used by those who should know better. I hate jargon. I hate the idea that rules govern language, though I do not expect you to find a split infinitive within this book. I hate Alastair Campbell. But most of all I hate Lynne Truss, who cornered the market in grumpy rants about the state of the nation's use of English, and makes this appear exactly what it is – a shameless piece of opportunism.

So how mega is this, like? I mean, like, is it awesome. In case you hadn't guessed, I hate that kind of language.

But I hate this kind of thing even more: the right to be offensive is always a prerequisite for public debate going forwards. This was written by someone who is supposed to be in the business of communication. How can people speak and write like this? Are they indifferent to the sound of language? This sort of thing – along with meeting Campbell or Truss – can ruin your day.

There are many types of attitude towards language. There are the slobs, the yobs, the nobs, the doubters and the pedants. I hate them all, though you might think I'm a pedant. But I'm not. I just implement the basic rules of grammar and use language correctly, unlike Campbell.

Why do people speak and write so badly? We need look no further than the appallingly indulgent attitudes towards education that we have fostered since the 60s. So, poor little diddums can't spell inoculate and doesn't know how to structure a basic sentence. Well, never mind, just do your best and we'll give you marks for trying. What kind of sloppiness is this? It's not fair on the kids and it's not fair on the rest of us who sometimes have to talk to them. I hate all this wishy-washy liberalism.

I want to stress again that I am not a pedant, though I would like to point out that I've been through every single one of that idiot Campbell's public statements and can state categorically that he doesn't understand the difference between disinterested and uninterested.

Now that I'm in the mood, let me tell you about some of the other things I hate. I hate people using verbs as nouns, I hate the way the Americans have corrupted the beauty of our language, I hate people using two words when just one will do, I hate politicians mangling words with their lies and obfuscations, and I hate Campbell.

Even the BBC has been guilty – in particular those cowering bureaucrats who gave in to the government bullies and started censoring the brilliant journalism of the *Today* programme. But let me end with these thoughts. One should not aim at being possible to understand but at being impossible to misunderstand. And if you bump into Alastair Campbell, give him a kicking. Metaphorically.

The digested read ... digested

The grumpiest man on radio stakes his claim to the title of grumpiest pedant on Grub St.

The digested read ...

Sport

Dazzler

Darren Gough with David Norrie

Lords 2000. Caddie, Corkie and I lay into the Windies. 54 all out. Unbelievable. 188 to get and we've levelled the series. Ramps fails, but then Athers and Vaughanie get us in a good position. Stewie, Knightie, Hickie and Chalky fail to capitalise, and we were 8 down with 28 to get when I joined Corkie at the crease. At that moment I'd rather have been anywhere else. It's moments like these you live for as a Test cricketer and I wouldn't have wanted to be anywhere else. I can't remember a thing from the time Corkie hit the winning runs to arriving back in Yorkshire the next morning.

I come from Yorkshire and I'm proud of it. Never let it be said that Darren Gough isn't proud of it, even though I've moved to Bucks. I came into the Yorkshire squad on the back of the YTS scheme, but I was fat and going nowhere until I met Anna, my wife. She taught me that a professional sportsman needs to look after himself. That's why I'll now only have five beers and a couple of glasses of wine the night before a Test. I got into the England side in 1994 and captured Mark Greatbatch in my first over. Who writes your scripts, Goughie?

I couldn't believe that Athers could be so stupid as to be caught with dirt in his pocket when we played the South Africans. Darren Gough would never do something like that. That Athers ball-tampering affair, what a load of fuss about nothing.

Even though I've been in and out of the side, through injury and ridiculous selection policies – that Illy was a prat – I've been financially well-off, thanks to my agent and my column in the *News of the World*. What a top bloke that David Norrie is. Drinks a bit, though.

I have a big confession to make. I thought the final Test at Centurion Park was going to be rained off, so I was still pissed when I got to the ground. Nas made me bowl 10 overs on the trot. You've got to respect him for that. Never let it be said that Darren Gough will ever be unprofessional again.

After our wins against Zimbabwe, the Windies, Pakistan and Sri Lanka, there's a new mood of optimism and confidence in the squad. With Darren Gough at his best, this team can compete with anyone. Bring on the Aussies, that's what Darren Gough says.

The digested read ... digested

Darren Gough says that Darren Gough plays lots of cricket and that anyone who says differently doesn't know Darren Gough very well.

Mr Nastase

Ilie Nastase

The press used to call me Nasty. But really I'm just an entertainer. Sure, I lost it a few times on the court, but that's because I'm an emotional man. I never intended to put off any of my opponents. Arthur Ashe – or Negroni, as I used to call him – was one of my best friends on tour and that should tell you that no one ever felt my antics were malicious.

I was born in Bucharest in 1946, and even as a child I lived for tennis. My parents were extremely supportive, but early on they decided not to come to any of my matches or take any interest in what I was doing. When I rung them to tell them I had won the French Open in 1973, my dad said, "What's that?" Deep down, I knew this was his way of showing he loved me.

Romanian players were rarely allowed to leave the country in the 60s and I never really learnt to develop my skills against better players until I was in my 20s. These days, a player is considered past it by the time he is 25! Even when we did leave the country, we were given little money, and Ion Tiriac and I would often sleep on the beach to make ends meet. Ion was much older than me and I used to look up to him, but once he realised I was a much better player than him he started to resent me and ignore me. But I've never held a grudge about this.

I was actually very shy as a young man and it was a long time before I dared to speak to girls. But once I was on the tour, I soon made up for it!! It's hard to resist when girls are throwing themselves at you. I was as happy to use them as they were happy to use me.

A big highlight was 1972. I won my first grand slam tournament and got married. Dominique was different to the other girls: she didn't sleep with me on the first date. She was also very rich, and our wedding was a real society event. We were blissfully happy, and she gave me a beautiful daughter, Natalie.

Before long the marriage was in trouble. Tennis kept us apart and I have to admit I wasn't entirely faithful. I wasn't proud of this, but I wasn't really that bothered either. My focus was on my tennis and having a good time entertaining my fans. By now I was top of the world rankings and earning a great deal.

Some players find it hard to carry on when they are no longer the best, but I was happy to play doubles and Masters events. I also got married to Alexandra, but that didn't last. She couldn't cope with my infidelity either. Now, though, I'm a changed man. My new wife, Amalia, would never let me be unfaithful.

Romania has seen a lot of changes in my lifetime. Under Ceausescu, I never flaunted my wealth, unlike someone called Ion. He went back after the fall of the regime and made a lot of money. His choice. I prefer to be remembered as Mr Nice Guy.

The digested read ... digested

A few lobs, several smashes and a bucketful of points scored as the 70s sex god self-serves for the match.

Paula: My Story So Far

Paula Radcliffe

I owe sport everything, which is why I'm happy to promote Cadbury's Get Active campaign. Kids these days aren't fat because they eat kilos of Dairy Milk: they're fat because they don't take any exercise. I also think Nike is a brilliant company. Now I've said my corporate thank-yous, I must thank my fabulous family, my gorgeous husband, Gary, my wonderful coach, Alex Stanton, and my incredible physiotherapist, Gerard Hartmann.

I had a fantastically happy childhood and my parents never had a cross word with one another except when they argued. We moved to Bedford when I was nine and I joined Bedford & County Athletics Club. We had a great group of young athletes. We all got on so well, though that changed when I started winning everything. Then some of the girls were beastly to me, but I still won. I'm pleased to say we're all the best of friends again. They're delighted I'm a millionaire and I'm delighted they've achieved nothing.

By the time I went to university, I had made something of a name for myself, having won the world junior cross-country championships. It was here that I met Gary. I fell for him immediately, though it took time for us to get together as he wasn't as keen on me as I was on him.

Gary: I thought Paula was OK when I met her but I didn't think she was that special. I had my own career to look after and reckoned I could do better. I know now I was a feckless arsehole and that I am very lucky Paula stays with me.

Seville was a real disappointment. Sydney was a real disappointment. Edmonton was a real disappointment.

Gary: I should never have shouted at Paula after the race. I'm lucky she's still talking to me.

I didn't want to be remembered as a gallant loser, and Gary and Alex had always suspected my real talent lay in the longer distances. I almost didn't get to the start of my first London Marathon as I was injured again. Thanks to Gerard I did, and all I remember is thinking how slowly I was running. That summer I went on to win the Commonwealth 5,000m and the European 10,000m. I was a drug-free winner on the track. Unlike some cheats.

Winning Chicago in a world-record time was the icing on the cake, though I could have gone faster if I hadn't had my period. And in London the next year I did.

Gary: She's just amazing. I'm so worthless.

Athens was a terrible ordeal. Winning an Olympic gold medal meant everything to me, and I felt awful having to drop out. Basically, my body couldn't cope with all the anti-inflammatories I was taking for an injury.

Gary: No one else would have got to the start line. Paula is a goddess.

There have been tears, but I'm a fighter, not a quitter, and now I feel great again.

The digested read ... digested

Just like Athens, this one's not worth finishing.

Team England Rugby: World Cup 2003

Forty-three players gathered in the Pennyhill Hotel in Bagshot at the start of England's World Cup campaign. After three more summer Tests, the squad would be whittled down to the final 30.

Eight of the squad were struck off the list after the first French game. "It's the toughest decision I've ever had to make, but I'm here to make tough decisions," said coach Clive Woodward.

The final five were struck off the list after the second French game. "It's the toughest decision I've ever had to make, but I'm here to make tough decisions," said coach Clive Woodward. The 30 chosen squad members were over the moon, but gutted for those who didn't make it.

Even though England were the overwhelming favourites against Georgia, no one was taking anything for granted. "We're not taking anything for granted," said everyone. After a convincing 84-6 win, the squad's main feeling was relief, though injury worries to Richard Hill and Matt Dawson were a concern. "We're relieved but concerned," said everyone.

England were far from convincing against South Africa but still came out convincing winners. "It's good we can still win convincingly when we are playing unconvincingly," said coach Clive Woodward. "Grunt," said skipper Martin Johnson.

England were far from convincing against Samoa but still came out convincing winners. "It's good we can still win convincingly when we are playing unconvincingly," said coach Clive Woodward. "Grunt," said skipper Martin Johnson.

England were far from convincing against Wales but still came out convincing winners. "It's good we can still win convincingly when we are playing unconvincingly," said coach Clive Woodward. "Grunt," said skipper Martin Johnson.

England met the mercurial French as the underdogs, but coach Clive Woodward was quietly confident. "I am quietly confident," he said. "Grunt," said skipper Martin Johnson.

A strong performance from the pack and the golden boot of St Jonny Wilkinson saw England crush their northern-hemisphere rivals in the Sydney rain.

It was the golden final. Australia, the bully-boy hosts, and our honest, God-fearing lads. Coach Clive Woodward was quietly confident. "I am quietly confident," he said loudly. "Grunt," said skipper Martin Johnson. By half-time England were well in control, but a series of inexplicable decisions by a poor South African referee let Australia back in.

Thirty seconds of extra time left and St Jonny's sublime drop kick sails effortlessly between the uprights. England are champions. "I feel a little daunted," said St Jonny, "but there are 15 in this marriage."

The digested read ... digested

England still win but fail to convert the magic of the Sydney night to the printed page.

Wisden Cricketers' Almanack 2003

Rock'n'roll, chaps. Michael Vaughan on the front cover? You ain't seen nothing yet. In 140 years' time we'll have a girl. Sorry for giving you the longest Wisden ever – there wasn't time to write a shorter one. Ha ha. Anyway, to sum up the year, those beastly Aussies, whom we have to pretend to admire but really hate, have carried all before them once more. What a marvellous, marvellous team of sledgers they are. Still, they'll have to do without that druggie Warney for a year.

On a more sombre note, we have to condemn the International Cricket Council for its pusillanimity in dealing with Zimbabwe. We are obviously extremely concerned about the atrocities that the Mugabe regime has inflicted on the black population, but it is the treatment of the white farming community we utterly abhor. Cricket owes its worldwide appeal to the British empire and it is within the sport's noblest traditions to support these last remaining colonials.

Who has seen the most Test matches? We decided to find out. John "Wooders" Woodcock weighed in with more than 400, but Richie Benaud tops the table with 484. The prize would have gone to Major "Bunter" Bufton, ex of the Free Foresters, who has been present at 534 matches. Unfortunately, because he has slept through most of them, he has had to be discounted.

Our five cricketers of the year are: Michael Vaughan, a marvellous player; Matthew Hayden, a marvellous player; Nasser Hussain, a marvellous player; Shaun Pollock, a marvellous player; Adam Hollioake, a marvellous player. Congratulations to all five of these marvellous players on a marvellous season.

Our hearts go out to Jonty Rhodes, who has retired from international cricket after sustaining an injury to his hand in the World Cup; he was a marvellous player and a committed Christian who found it in his heart to forgive Hansie Cronje when others wouldn't. He will be sorely missed.

England v India, fourth Test. This match was the thriller that never was. After England compiled a massive 515, India replied with 508. There was just time for England's openers to race to 114 in the second innings before rain cut short proceedings on the final day. Nevertheless, it was an absorbing end to an absorbing series, leaving the two teams poised at 1-1.

Azerbaijan: Despite financial hardship, Baku CC enjoyed an extremely successful year. Obituaries: Thomas "Corky" Bullard, who died on 11 September 1995. His death was not immediately noticed in cricket circles as members of the Garrick Club assumed he was sleeping off another of his legendary lunches. Corky turned out once for Old Carthusians in 1953, scoring 1 and taking 0 for 92 in seven overs.

The digested read ... digested

1,760 pages for £35 declared (Tim de Lisle retired hurt 1).

Selective
memories

Experience

Martin Amis

I write both to commemorate my father and to set the record straight. This will involve me in the indulgence of certain bad habits. Name dropping is one of them. But I've been indulging in this, in a way, ever since I first said "Mart".

There will be no point-scoring, valued reader, though if you're reading this, Jules, I'd like to say that it was you who turned away from me, not I who turned away from you. So you can fuck right off for a start. And as for you, Thersites Eric, who demeaned and defiled our family after Kingsley's death, I'll deal with you and the toiling small-holders of the Fourth Estate in a 10-page appendix.

Rather, this is the journey through the unconscious, the "un" conscious, the un, of how the fledgling Osric became Hamlet, Prince of Westbourne Grove. It is here in the world of un, that murky novelist's landscape, where experience is collected, connections are made and communion is freely given and received. Here we will find the pain schedule, the climacteric collision of the missing and the lost, the Delilahs and the Lucys, and the loves that come and go. There is no morality. What must be must be. All we can do is rage and hurt and pay the bill.

It is the late 1970s. The gross of condoms that Kingsley gave me and Phillip have long since been used. Many times over. I am looking at a photo of a two-year-old girl, another version of myself.

"Do you think she might be mine?" I asked my mother.

"Definitely."

"What shall I do?"

"Nothing."

But I didn't do nothing. I didn't see her or take an interest in her, obviously. No, I did something more profound and important. I wrote about her. *In scribendo veritas*. A careful reading of my novels, from the publication of *Success* in 1978 onwards, will reveal a stream of lost or wandering and putative or fugitive fathers. So Delilah and I were always together, our inner-selves linked in un-ness, un-needing of a corporeal presence.

The mid-90s were my lurid years, using lurid strictly according to the condensed epic poem of the Fowlers' article in the *COD*. A mid-life crisis is critical in a man; a man who reaches his forties without one has no concept of the continuum of being. The beginnings and the endings. And all things must end. My marriage to Antonia was ending, my teeth had prematurely resigned and Kingsley was creeping to his reluctant adieu. Only Saul, the world's other great novelist, could truly comfort.

But in the endings there are also joys. There is you, Isabel, and Delilah, who have come back to me. *Immenso giubilo*. I worried that you and the boys would not get on. Ridiculous. And even with no genetic barrier between me and my own mortality, there is a freedom in being orphaned. My tennis has got much, much better since Kingsley died. There. My experience is told. Now there is the living to be done.

The digested read ... digested

Brilliantly written, highly selective, episodic portrayal of a life well-thought but only half felt.

The Centre of the Bed: An Autobiography

Joan Bakewell

The left-hand side or the right-hand side? It was so hard to choose when there were three or four of us in the marriage. Now I'm happy with the centre. For some reason I am reminded of Carpaccio's St Ursula. Probably because I can't resist showing off my erudition.

I was born in Stockport in 1933. I never liked the name Joan and I always wished I had been called Diana. Or maybe that's my memory playing up. It's so hard to be sure. I want to write lovingly of my parents every bit as much as I want to name-drop Proust and Nabokov. But I find it hard with my mother because she was a miserable depressive who never got any help.

We went to Argentina, which is on the eastern seaboard of South America, just before the war. And then we came back. During the war I prayed for the Germans to win because the church commanded us to love our enemies. It may surprise you to learn that I was the school swot and I won a place at Cambridge.

How free I felt there and how wonderful to meet all sorts of other brilliant people with whom I would go on to work. I revelled in the new feminism of Simone de Beauvoir! So much so that I was married to Michael and bringing up two children in next to no time. Dizzy days.

I met a stranger at a party in north London and asked him his name. There was a long pause, pregnant with possibilities. "Ah," I said, breaking the silence. "You must be Harold Pinter." We immediately embarked on a long and passionate affair that was celebrated in Harold's remarkable play *The Betrayal*.

Michael discovered our affair but was happy for it to continue as he was having a few of his own. What times the 1960s were. I soon started working on the new *Late Night Line Up* in the first days of BBC2, and it was wonderful to work with so many of the most gifted people of my generation.

It was then that Frank Muir called me The Thinking Man's Crumpet. People often ask me if I minded, and the truth is that sometimes I did and sometimes I didn't. But I always thought it was better than being labelled The Thinking Man's Ear Trumpet.

Michael and I eventually divorced. It had become increasingly difficult to stop my affair with Harold becoming public knowledge, as one of us was acquiring an international reputation and the other was a playwright.

I was then dropped by the BBC, married Jack Emery, another depressive. I do seem to pick them. He had an affair and we split up and I did a lot more fascinating television shows, such as *Heart of the Matter*. Now I'm 70, which I'm told is the new 50. Rock'n'roll, girls and boys.

The digested read ... digested

The Princess of Hearts of early BBC2.

Widower's House

John Bayley

Gosh. What? Sorry, I was dozing off again. The dust has rather been gathering around me since Iris died. Actually, come to think of it, the dust was gathering while Iris was still alive. I like our dust. I've only got to look at the grime on my trouser bottoms, and I remember the laughter Iris and I shared.

Why do people always want to look after widowers? I want to be left alone with my memories, not humoured out of them. Grief is self-centred. What was it Hardy said? No matter. It'll come back to me in a minute. Anyway, here I am in Norfolk, after a ghastly drive from Oxford, being force-fed a casserole by Margot.

"You need me to tidy up your house," she barked.

I didn't need her for anything, but I was too timid to say so, and a few weeks later she swept into Oxford.

"Don't mind my being here, Johnny. I thought this might be comforting for both of us," she mewed, as her grey hair fell across my pillow. She was only trying to be kind.

There was a knock on the door. It was Mella, one of my former students. "I've brought you a pork pie," she said, before getting to work with the vacuum cleaner.

She was rather a long time upstairs, and I found her lying fully clothed on the bed. We were soon both naked. Mella was rather scrawny but I think Iris might have approved.

Mella was a single parent, and we spent many an hour discussing her son, Damian or Darren. She even became friends with Margot and I began to suspect them of a little lesbian tendresse.

"She doesn't have a son, you know," Margot confided in a letter.

Mella stormed out the house when I showed her the letter. Perhaps I should have followed, and I wondered whether she would become a prostitute or drug addict.

Still it was nice to be left to my shadowy world of bereavement.

"I'm back," said Mella, some months later. "I'm off," I replied, rushing out the door. "I'm going to Lanzarote to marry Audi. If I can find my passport, that is."

Is that enough? Has the cheque from the Telegraph cleared? My memory is beginning to play tricks. Grief does that, you know. What a silly old duffer I am.

The digested read ... digested

John Bayley enjoys the comfort of strangers after Iris Murdoch's death. Or, there again, maybe he doesn't.

A Cook's Tour

Anthony Bourdain

Yo, motherfuckers. I'm sitting in the bush with Charlie, deep in the Mekong Delta, drinking hooch. My hosts, VC war heroes, pass me the duck. I chomp through its bill, before cracking open the skull and scooping the brains out.

When you've just had a big score with an obnoxious and over-testosteroned account of your life, your publishers tend to fall for any dumb-ass plan. So when I told them I wanted to go round the world eating all sorts of scary food in a search for the perfect meal, they just said, "Where do we sign?"

Y'know, most of us in the west have lost contact with the food we eat. It comes merchandised and homogenised. The same goes for chefs. Cooking isn't about knocking up a few wussy monkfish terrines out of fillets that have been delivered to the kitchen door it's about bad-ass guys going deep into their souls and looking their ingredients in the eye.

Which is why I am in Portugal, outside the barn while Jose and Francisco restrain several hundredweight of screaming pig. I unsheathe my knife, bury it deep into the neck and draw it firmly towards me. The pig looks at me in surprise and fury. I lick the blood from my arms, make another incision and rip out the guts. The women pan-fry the spleen. It's indescribably good.

I take my brother to France to look for the oysters and foie gras of my youth. I only find memories of my dead father. That's not what being a chef is all about. Cut to Mexico. The restaurant owner's 10-year-old pet iguana hoves into view. Big mistake. Its meat is tough and the claws are inedible; this is more like it.

I'm a sucker for sushi, but my main reason for being in Japan was to eat fugu, the puffer fish whose deadly nerve toxins in the liver kill scores of devotees a year. I watched Mr Yoshida prepare the fish. He was too clean, too careful. Not even the hint of a psychotropic high. Fuck that.

So off to Nam for fried birds' heads and monkey steaks. But even this wasn't really hard. I needed to be in Cambodia, driving along the heavily mined highway to Pailin, Kalashnikov on my knee and with skulls the only road signs. The restaurant owner brought in a live cobra and slit its throat in front of me. He wrenched out the heart and placed it, still beating, on my plate. "Make you strong," he said. I do feel strong. I have my machete. I'm in the bamboo plantation. And there's the giant panda.

The digested read ... digested

Colonel Kurtz Bourdain goes deep into the heart of darkness and returns the sole survivor of the culinary bloodbath.

Down Under

Bill Bryson

Gee. Australia is a very, very big country and no one knows much about it. Especially Americans. Which makes it the ideal spot for another of my homey little travelogues.

So what else can I tell you by way of background? Well, it's very, very big, there are loads of deadly creepy-crawlies (Yuck!!), it was colonised by convicts (imagine!!) and the present inhabitants can be fairly chippy. But let me say, right here, right now, that I love Australians.

So where shall I start my trip? A colour magazine is paying me to turn around a quick piece on the Sydney-to-Perth Express so that seems as good a place as any. The train stops at Broken Hill. Pause, while I read up the history books and repeat some amusing anecdotes. We go for a day's driving out in the bush and when I get back I look at the map and see we've hardly moved out of Broken Hill.

Gee, it's a big country. The next leg of the train ride goes smoothly. I go in the cab for a bit and then I slum it in third class for a couple of hours. Scar-ry. And this is Perth, but I can't stick around as I've got another job to do in the Middle East.

Hi. I'm back. But not for long as I've only got a month and I'm hoping to cover the whole of the south-east corner, so we'd better get going.

Hey, look, there's a pet food shop that sells porno out the back. That's really neat. And, wow, the cricket on the car radio really cracks me up. "I wonder if he'll chance an offside drop scone here or go for the quick legover." Crazy. Why can't all these guys play exactly the same games as the rest of us? Such as American football.

Here's Adelaide (pause for some historical anecdotes) and there's the fascinating museum. Unfortunately it's closed for the day and my schedule's too tight to hang on.

Oh, and that might have been Melbourne and, wow, I must be back in Sydney and I'm outta here.

Right, I'm back for a few days so we're going up north. Ah, it's the rainy season. I hadn't thought of that. So Cairns is as far as I get. Let's take the plane to Darwin (not very nice) and drive to Alice Springs. Now, I'll just nip to Ayers Rock for a couple of hours as I've forgotten to book a hotel, then it's over to Perth for a suntan and Bob's your uncle. My cheque's in the bank.

The digested read ... digested

Big Bill goes walkabout and sees everything and nothing. A snake bite would have put everyone out of their misery.

Under No Illusions

Paul Daniels

Whenever Debbie and I give a party for our envious showbiz pals in our beautiful riverside home with 12 acres of formal gardens and stunning woodlands, I think of how far I have come from my humble Yorkshire origins.

My mum and dad were brilliant at everything. We were very poor, mind, but we never complained about our lot. We loved our nigger brown door – you could use words like that back then and no one took offence. Happy days.

I became interested in magic at an early age when I took out a book on the subject from the library. I must give it back some time!!!!! It's the way I tell 'em.

National Service made a man of me and taught me respect. The government should bring it back for the youth of today. Only for men, though. Soldiering isn't for women or poofs.

I couldn't get beyond kissing in my teens. But after I picked up a prostitute in Hong Kong there was no looking back and I had dozens of affairs throughout my unhappy marriage to Jackie. I guess I'm not small in all departments. D'you geddit? Small ...

All this time I was doing the clubs in the evening and working for the council in the day. It was tough but worth it, as everyone agreed I was the best magician in the world. Well, nearly everyone. The odd person didn't understand what I was doing; they've probably gone on to be big in BBC light entertainment!!!

In the early 70s, I decided to concentrate on show BUSINESS rather than SHOW business and it soon paid off. I'm very, very rich now and I'm great to my family. I even let my brother, Trevor, drive my Ferrari sometimes. It does sadden me, though, that some people have said they couldn't work with me because I was a conceited know-all.

Throughout the 70s, my TV career took off and in 1979 we began the first of FIFTEEN series of *The Paul Daniels Show*. You heard me, FIFTEEN. It was here that I met a petite, lithe dancer called Debbie. She didn't fancy me at first but I took her on a boat and tidal waves of passion soon followed. Tidal waves. Geddit?

We're a great team. Apart from my son, whose problems are absolutely nothing to do with me, life is great and I could give you anecdote after anecdote of my amusing showbiz lifestyle. In fact, I will.

The digested read ... digested

Magician's autobiography that ought to have been sawn in half and made to disappear. Will you like it? Not a lot.

Chronicles: Volume 1
Bob Dylan

Lou Levy, top man at Leeds Music Publishing, took me up in a taxi to West 70th Street. Outside the wind was blowing.

"Columbia have high hopes for you," he said.

I'd met John Hammond at Columbia the previous week.

"Howdya get to town?" he asked.

"Jumped a freight train."

It was pure hokum. But who wants truth, when you can buy the dream?

I was staying in The Village with Ray Van Ronk. Outside the wind was blowing. Ray was like a wolf, living like he was hiding out. It was said that the second world war spelled the end of the Age of Enlightenment, but I wouldn't have known it. I was still in it. I'd read the stuff. Voltaire, Rousseau, Locke ... it was like I knew those guys.

I usually started a book at the middle. It was like I was looking for the education I never got. Thucydides, Gogol, Faulkner. They were like a freeway to my mind.

I wanted to cut a record. But not a 45. I went down to play a song for Woody Guthrie. "You brought that song to life," he said.

I'd been in a motorcycle accident. I just wanted out of the rat race. Journalists, promoters, fans: they were all calling me the tortured conscience of America. I never planned to be an icon. I was just a singer writing songs that made some kind of sense to me. Outside the wind was blowing.

People told me what my lyrics meant. It was news to me. One album was supposedly intensely autobiographical. Let them think so. I knew it was based on a bunch of Chekhov short stories. I just wanted to escape with my wife and raise my kids like any other American.

I was on tour with Tom Petty, but I felt I was going through the motions. I couldn't connect with my songs or find a voice. I'm gonna retire at the end of this, I thought. I'm burnt out.

My manager told me to take time out to rehearse with the Grateful Dead, but I had reached the point when I opened my mouth and nothing came out. The terror was overwhelming, but then, from nowhere, a sound emerged. It wasn't a pretty sound, but it was one I recognised. My songs had come back to me.

I was having lunch with the popular Irish singer Bono. We looked deep into each other's reflector shades and liked what we saw.

"God wants you to record with Daniel Lanois," he said.

It was the first Danny had heard of it, but we started to lay some tracks. Outside the wind was blowing. But we stitched and pressed and packed and drove.

John Pankake told me I was trying to be too much like Woody Guthrie. I changed my style. You're now trying to be too much like Robert Johnson. The folk music scene was a paradise, and like Adam I had to leave.

The digested read ... digested

The answers are still blowing in the wind.

The Way We Wore

Robert Elms

The whistle was correct in every detail: petrol blue, wool and mohair. "It's all the go," said my mother, giving me an excuse to use the word "idiolectically" and show I'm not just an air-headed fashionista but an intellectual cultural commentator.

I've always loved clothes; even now I can't help admiring my row of handmade suits in their purpose-built closet. It's not an empty, narcissistic love, but one built on an appreciation of their emblematic significance in Marxist orthodoxy.

Everyone living in our working-class area of Notting Dale was a tasty geezer. We ducked; we dived; we bought clothes. We had a rugged proletarian attitude to money that produced an authentic style quite different from that of the effete middle classes.

I was just six when our working-class phone rang and I was told my dad had died. I was crushed by the sense that this great bear of a tasty geezer would never help me rearrange my wardrobe. Shortly afterwards our house was compulsorily purchased and we were relocated to Burnt Oak, another hard, uncompromisingly working-class area in north-west London and by the age of 10 I had adopted the skinhead uniform, though I later became concerned when it was appropriated by the far right.

My brother, Reggie, did some well-hard time inside, though he had to wear ill-fitting prison clothes, and I was left to carve my own way through the boutique of life. I developed an eclectic, working-class musical taste to match my dress sense, and I sneered at John Lennon. Imagine no possessions? What did Lennon know about the lumpenproletariat?

By the mid-70s the icy blast of working-class punk rebellion – far removed from the middle-class appropriation of New Wave – was cranked up to full mixed metaphors, and I was first in line to pay too much for bondage trousers. It was too much for the pseudo-socialists at the LSE, who couldn't cope with the realism of a genuine member of the working classes. While they worried about the pettiness of the three-day week, I was getting involved in the hardcore politics of the club scene.

On leaving the LSE, I became a music journalist; this was the frontline in the war against bourgeois oppression. Very quickly I became recognised as a figurehead for the New Romantics: I dreamed up the name for Spandau Ballet on a visit to East Germany and I still believe my article in the *Face* on the importance of vintage denim was instrumental in bringing down Thatcher.

My wardrobe grew even bigger than my ego as I got more famous. I became a TV star, went out with Sade and wrote a novel based on my life in clothes. And now that I fancy another suit, I've persuaded a publisher to give me an advance for rewriting it as autobiography.

The digested read ... digested

Lightweight? Suits you, sir.

My Life in Orange

Tim Guest

I felt alone, different from all my friends. They all had great careers. And then I realised I could trade on my childhood. *Fever Pitch* meets Bhagwan. What more could a publisher want? My very own autobiography before the age of 30. I was going to be the talk of Radio 4.

My mum and dad met at a party, got stoned and fell in love. Not long after, I was born. Six months later, she met someone else. I stayed with my father and then she came back and we moved into a commune in Leeds. Three years later she turned orange, changed her name to Vismaya and fell in love with Sujan. She then moved to the ashram in Pune without me.

Look, I know the orange people were basically sad wackos who couldn't cope with real life and couldn't spot a fraud when they saw one, but I now need to include lots of dreary details about Bhagwan to pad out the book and give it some credibility. Bhagwan was born ... He did this and that ... Lots of sex and meditation ... Rolls-Royces ...

That's enough of that. Like many four-year-olds my prime concern was to get my hands on as many sweets as possible, but deep down I was an extremely tortured, sensitive child, yearning to be loved and held, yet pulled in different directions by parents on opposite sides of the world.

How I longed to punish the children who stole my toys and the mother who put her enlightenment before her only child. See in this photograph how lost and frightened, yet somehow strangely beautiful, I appear. My eyes are looking far into the distance –

to my literary career. So I chose to say nothing and smile. Until now.

The Bhagwan looked at me once and later sent me a letter, giving me sannyas and telling me my name was Yogesh. I counted myself fortunate. My mother left Pune to set up the Medina ashram in Suffolk, though I saw as little of her there as I had in India. Cue more sex and meditation. Sometimes I would go and stay with my dad in California where we would go to Disneyland. And then I would come back. Still I had no sense of belonging.

My mother was invited to stay at the new Rajneeshpuram in Oregon. It was a lot like being in India or Suffolk. Which was a bit boring really. Sometimes we would go back to England and once we were even asked to go to Germany. But that was like everywhere else, too. The only thing that wasn't like being on the ashram was the time spent with my dad, but that, too, felt familiar after a while.

Towards the end, various ashram leaders started behaving like autocrats, but my mother wasn't unduly concerned and neither was I. I was too locked into my despair. Bhagwan and the others were eventually arrested for fraud, but most of his followers were too zonked to care. One day my mum was an orange person, the next she wasn't. Then we had a few arguments and here we are.

The digested read ... digested

As toxic as you'd expect from Agent Orange.

Slipstream

Elizabeth Jane Howard

I was born a long time ago and I really can't remember very much about my early childhood except all the things I've remembered. It was decreed that I should go away to school, but I never made any friends and was very sickly, so I was sent home to our tiny eight-bedroomed mansion in Notting Hill.

On Christmas day my mother and father slipped out of the house for a two-week holiday without telling me. My father was a charismatic man who took a great interest in me, though he did once overstep the mark and abuse me.

I always thought I was very ugly and so when Peter Scott asked me out I went to bed with him. Peter had to go away when the war against a man called Hitler started. He came back and told me the man he was in love with had found another woman, so he would make do with me. I felt terrific and we were soon married. We had a daughter, Nicola, whom I handed over to the nanny.

In 1943, I started an affair with Peter's brother, Wayland. Peter wasn't happy and bedded me doggedly every night. I then met Phillip Lee and we had an exciting affair until he ran off with someone else.

I left Peter in 1947 after Robert Aickman told me he fancied me. When this affair ended I started another with the married financier, Michael Behrens, and had my first novel published by Mr Cape. Michael sent me on holiday with his friend and I slept with him, too.

Arthur Koestler invited me out so I had an affair with him, and the same thing happened with Laurie Lee, Cecil Day-Lewis and

Ken Tynan. I then married a con man called Jim because the president of the Ouspensky Society told me to.

While I was organising the Cheltenham Literary Festival I met Kingsley, and it was about now that I remembered I had forgotten Nicola. I taught Mart how to read, but then Kingsley fell out of love with me.

Cecil died, swiftly followed by my mother, Elizabeth, Victor and Kingsley. I felt very alone, even though I wrote a few more books, had some therapy and moved to Suffolk.

A man started writing to me so I had sex with him. Shortly afterwards I got cancer. I am now very old and quite well-off, but not so rich that I don't need to write this book.

The digested read ... digested

Dial V for victim.

The Wages of Spin

Bernard Ingham

As a Yorkshireman, and proud of it, I'm not afraid to speak my mind. And I can tell you that when Labour was re-elected in 2001, the cynic in me wondered whether we weren't seeing the death of British politics. The reason for this was Alastair Campbell and the detestable culture of spin.

It has often been said that it was I who was largely responsible for creating this atmosphere when I served as Margaret Thatcher's press officer. To which I have just two words in reply. Bunkum and balderdash. I have never, ever sought the limelight, and as the ministers whom I am proud to have served will tell you, my only goal throughout my long and distinguished career has been the dissemination of the truth. And if I did ever seek publicity, I did so out of duty. By Jove, yes.

I was just a humble member of the Government Information Service when Margaret did me the honour of asking me to become her press secretary. Some have accused me of having got so close to her that I joined the Conservative party. To which I have just two words in reply. Bunkum and balderdash. It is true we did become enormously close over the many years we worked together, and I am proud to have provided her with some of her best soundbites, but at no time was I anything less than impartial or professional.

We always observed the formalities. "Bernard," she would say. "You are my rock." At which comment I would always click my heels and salute with a swift, "Danke, mein Fuhrer."

If I was a little evasive in my early days in office – sorry, as the prime minister's press secretary – it was not because I was trying to conceal the truth, but because I wasn't being told anything. All I ever worked for was to make journalists' lives easier. When the hordes outside Downing Street became a scrum, I herded them all into a little pen to make them feel more secure. And I worried that the smaller ones at the back wouldn't be able to hear Margaret properly, so I got her a lectern and a microphone so she could hector audibly.

I also rebut any suggestions that I ever leaked anything, especially over Westland.

Great, great commentators such as Robin Oakley have said I was the greatest civil servant ever to walk through the doors of No 10. Only a man of my stature could have been press secretary and head of the GIS at the same time without compromising his independence.

Since 1997 it has been all downhill with special advisers and spin. I despair. And to those hacks on the Mirror and the Independent who ever dared criticise me, I say: "Show your faces in Hebden Bridge and I'll bloody well have yer."

The digested read ... digested

The pot calls the kettle black.

Woman of Today

Sue MacGregor

Be quiet while I'm interrupting. That's better. Now sit down and listen carefully.

My parents were both called MacGregor. That's quite interesting, isn't it? For my first seven years we lived in Beaconsfield, only 100 yards away from Enid Blyton. One day I knocked on her door and got her to sign copies of her books. Some 15 years later I knocked on her door again and she agreed to let me interview her.

SM: You've written a lot of books.

EB: Yes.

SM: How do you do it?

EB: I sit down with a typewriter until I've finished.

Fascinating stuff.

We moved to South Africa when I was seven, but don't worry we were liberals and we did know Helen Suzman. I moved back to England when I was 18 and got my first job with the BBC as a typist, but I soon returned to South Africa where I quickly became a presenter for the radio magazine show, *Woman's World*. I couldn't believe my luck. How am I doing? Is this interesting?

By 1967, the situation in South Africa had become far worse and I happily came back to England and auditioned for the BBC. I soon started work on *The World at One*, or *Wato* as we called it. How we laughed about that. Soon, though, I took over at *Woman's Hour*, which I really enjoyed.

My editor says this is all a bit dull and I need to spice it up a bit. Well, I did have an affair with Leonard Rossiter. He made me feel very happy, but I did feel a little guilty. I was upset when he died, though. I also got very close to Robin Day and I was upset when he died, too. Is this more like it?

I eventually moved on to the *Today* programme. There were a lot of competing egos there, I can tell you. Brian Redhead, John Humphrys, Peter Hobday, Jim Naughtie. There was always intense rivalry for the big 8.10 interview. We had our moments off air, though.

I'm afraid the rest has to be a bit controversial. John Birt wasn't the right man for the BBC. There, I've said it, and I don't mind sticking my neck out.

The editor liked that last bit and has told me to stick to issues. Um. Let me see. Did you know that women still get a rough deal in broadcasting? Mm, you probably did. Ah well, that'll have to do as I'm retiring now. Must go.

The digested read ... digested

The woman of *Today* signs off to become woman of yesterday.

Publisher

Tom Maschler

I was 27 when Hemingway killed himself. His death is the only regret of my magnificent career. Had he known I had just joined Cape and was to have become his editor, I am sure he would still be alive today. I do take some comfort, though, from having created his lasting masterpiece, *A Moveable Feast*, from the shambolic ramblings he left behind.

My father was a publisher and my mother wasn't. That's enough about them. I never saw the need to go to university, as everyone I met always assumed I had already been, and national service was the only interruption to my literary pre-eminence.

There is one anecdote from this period I never tire of telling. I was once mistakenly taken to a military asylum; inside there were 13 men who all thought they were Jesus Christ. Fortunately, I was able to inform the authorities that none of the men looked remotely like my son.

The Italians failed to recognise my talent for film, so I joined André Deutsch in London. Here I advised authors to find a better publishing house. After a little while, I moved on to MacGibbon & Kee, where I commissioned *Declaration*, the most important book of the 1950s. This was not my only brilliant decision. I also bought a house in Primrose Hill for £1,200; it's now worth £1.2m.

My genius came to the notice of Allen Lane and I joined Penguin. Here I commissioned the most important books of the era. Martin Browne impertinently took the credit for *New English Dramatists*, but when I pointed out his hubris he was happy to defer to me on later editions.

Allen was not happy when I joined Cape in 1960, but the time was right for me to change publishing. In America everyone was desperate to meet me. Wolfe, Roth, Heller, Pynchon: they were all nobodies until I worked my magic. The only person to resist my charms was Bellow, but that was maybe just as well as he wasn't very good.

Back in England I championed all the greatest writers of the age, though they were very raw talents when they came to my attention. Barnes, Amis and McEwan could barely write their own names yet I was able to spot a speck of promise and nurture it into something more substantial, and I am very touched they recognise how much they owe to me.

I am delighted to have worked with so many prize-winning authors, but my talent has extended into all areas of publishing – picture books, cookery books and children's books. There is not a bestselling writer alive who is not happy to call me their friend. I even published Jeffrey Archer, the only man I've met as conceited as myself.

I consider myself lucky to have had such a career, but mostly I consider the literary world lucky to have found such a colossus.

The digested read ... digested

The biggest ego on Grub Street branches out into vanity publishing.

Things My Mother Never Told Me

Blake Morrison

Hark! Dost the gentle wheezing from my mother's chest grow
  ever softer?
Is that her spirit passing now or has it passed long since?
Still her breath and let it ne'er be said
I missed a chance to be a poet of the dead

The phone rings. It's the nursing home to say my mother's end
is nigh. We have been here before, so many false goodbyes, that
I find myself wondering whether I have time to finish a review.
But duty – such a mean-spirited word, but surely none else will
do – forces me out the house. I make it to her bedside with just
40 minutes to spare.

Later that evening, my sister Gill and I go to our mother's home.
We drink too much and row as orphans often do.

"Mam always loved me more than you," pouts Gill.

"Well I'm going to write a book about her," I reply. "Then
we'll see who the public thinks loved her more."

Looking through my mother's possessions, I am struck by how
little I knew of her. Unlike my father, who loved attention
and would have adored my bestselling book about him, my
mother was a shadowy, private figure who liked nothing more
than not to be noticed. So obviously she would have hated
the idea of this book, but that should not stop me, I thought.
Would William Leith fail to exploit his family for a large
cheque? Of course not. And am I not a man of equal sensitivity
and depth?

Why did my mother not tell me she had so many siblings? Was she ashamed of them and of her roots? Or was she merely worried that if I discovered I had so many relations I would write about them, too?

I feel guilty reading through my parents' love letters. Have I mentioned how guilty I feel about invading their privacy? See how my father refuses to call her Agnes, or even Gennie. "I will call you Kim," he says, and she accepts it.

There are times in their courtship when their love seems to be waning and I feel my very existence coming into doubt. But of course I was, so even a few literary stylistic tics cannot generate much excitement in the story. I know as little of my mother now as when I started. She let my father walk all over her and now she's let me do the same.

The digested read ... digested

Attention all Morrisons. If you value your privacy don't even think of dying before Blake.

Being Jordan

Katie Price

I've been called a slapper, a freak and a bimbo. But there's more to me than that: I'm also obsessed with celebrity. This is my story.

I had the happiest childhood any girl could want. My dad left when I was three, but I never missed him because he had never been around much. My mum was amazing and I was thrilled when she met someone else and had another child.

By the time I was 13 years old I knew I was destined to be famous, and even though the first photographer to take glamour shots of me turned out to be a paedophile, I was determined not to let anything stop me from becoming a model and a pop star.

My first boyfriend was called Jeff. I made him wait a month before I let him have sex with me. I make everyone wait a month to prove I'm not easy. Except for the blokes I shag a bit sooner! Jeff had a small willy and I never really enjoyed the sex.

Modelling for the Sun sent my career stratospheric, and I decided to trade in Jeff for a boyfriend more fitting to my celebrity status, and soon I ended up with first a Gladiator and then Dane Bowers, a pop star from a band no one remembers any more. I hate the way both men have betrayed me by selling their stories. I would never do that. Both men had rather nondescript willies and they made me partake in unusual sexual practices. I should have left both earlier, but I'm a very loyal woman.

I want this next bit on the record. I've had three operations to enhance my breasts. They look lovely and I've never regretted it, though my back's started to play up a bit.

I nearly went out with Teddy Sheringham, but he went cold when the papers found out about us. I did meet David Beckham, though. He held my hand while Posh wasn't looking. She's really rough without make-up.

My career was going from strength to strength, and I started dating Dwight Yorke. He was a real pig. He didn't fancy me when my legs were heavily bruised from liposuction. Then I found out I was pregnant and he didn't want to know. So I went off to do a Playboy shoot. All the bunnies shave their bush, just like me, and they all said how natural my breasts look. Then when I was six months pregnant I started shagging Gareth Gates as it looked good on my CV. He had a small willy.

I was gutted when I discovered Harvey was blind, but felt sure he would have wanted me to go to LA to publicise my Playboy shoot. So I did. I was very distressed when paparazzi took photos of me, wearing a bikini, leading Harvey on a horse.

I'm A Celebrity was amazing. Peter Andre is the man of my dreams. He could launch my pop career. I'm tired of being "the girl who gets her tits out". Maybe it's time to drop my knickers.

The digested read ... digested

The only time you'll feel sorry for Dwight Yorke.

Richard & Judy: the Autobiography

Richard Madeley & Judy Finnigan

Judy: Since appearing on *This Morning* our marriage has been described as a sham, I've been called an alcoholic and Richard has been accused both of beating me up and shoplifting. To cap it all, my perfectly normal women's problems gave rise to the rumour I was terminally ill. None of this is true. We are a very close, happy family and our marriage is very, very strong. Is that the sort of thing you wanted, Richard?

Richard: Gosh, hi, super. You know the basis of any strong relationship is trust and, well, we're so trusting we haven't even bothered to read each other's chapters. So, Judy, stick to what I told you or I'll break your legs. Only joking.

Judy: I had an extremely close relationship with David, my first husband, but then we drifted apart after the twins arrived and I went back to work.

Richard: Anyone looking at my bedroom when I was a kid would have guessed I wanted to be a fighter pilot. And as soon as I made enough money as a cub reporter I bought a Triumph Spitfire. Tally ho, chaps.

Judy: I didn't think Richard was my type at first but there was chemistry between us. He was very mature for a 12-year-old.

Richard: Judy's first words to me were, "Hi, I'm your mummy." I thought, "Phwooar, I'm in here. Got any sweets?"

Judy: We cemented our relationship by having two beautiful children.

Richard: Oh yeah, we had a couple of kids. They're great, you know.

Judy: I'll tell you why I love Richard. He's steadfast and honest, though he can be a bit bumptious. People often say I'm brighter than him because I went to university and he didn't, but I'm sure he will when he finishes his A-levels.

Richard: I didn't nick anything from Tesco. I just strolled out without paying. No big deal, right. Just like scrumping.

Judy: We struggled a bit when we moved to London from Manchester. But Hampstead is very nice.

Richard: Did you see the tits on Judy when her dress came undone at the Baftas? Fan-bloody-tastic.

Judy: In our heart of hearts, we knew it was time to leave *This Morning*.

Richard: Look at all that lovely wonga.

The digested read ... digested

The life and times of Britain's first couple of the TV sofa.

Bravemouth

Pamela Stephenson

I hated finishing Billy. The writing of it had allowed me to overstate my own contribution to Billy's life and career, and for a while at least I had been the media equal of my brave, gentle and heroic husband. But now I could feel myself slipping back into the shadows once more.

Others had clearly enjoyed Billy, too, and I was immensely touched by the letters that found their way to me. Typical of these were, "Reading Billy cured my cancer" and "Reading Billy enabled me to find weapons of mass destruction."

Buoyed by these responses, I resolved to write another book, chronicling the world's most brilliant comic through his 60th year. Fortunately, this most warm and loving man embraced the idea wholeheartedly.

"You can do what you fucking want, Pamsy," he said. How typical of such a tortured soul to express his enthusiasm like this.

"I've just dyed my fucking beard purple," he shrieked, when we met up again several months later at one of the many castles we own around the world. I'd got used to Billy's hugely endearing eccentricities over the year, but I needed all my psychoanalytic training to cope with the colour of his beard. It would have been easy to dismiss it as the act of a narcissistic show-off, but I knew it was his way of confronting all those who had abused him as a child.

For much of the year I was in LA, India, New Zealand and Fiji so I didn't have much contact with Billy. I hope you don't mind me filling in with a few reminiscences of these places to pass the time.

Ah, Billy's back and I feel myself coming alive again. It took some convincing to persuade Billy it was worth letting me spend several million pounds on flying in all his working-class friends, such as Dame Judi Dench and Prince Charles, for his birthday party on our Scottish estate. Poor darling, hunted, big-hearted man.

The next time Billy and I met was at another party I had arranged for him. This time it was on an enchanted Pacific island and I had again flown in all his ordinary showbiz friends. "See how much they love you," I said. "You are a worthwhile human being."

Billy left the next day to film an advert for the lottery. How noble of Billy to remain true to his Glaswegian roots by persuading people to part with money they can't spare for a prize they won't win!

"I'm in fucking Japan, Pamsy, making a fucking movie with Tom fucking Cruise," he yelled down the phone. "Would you fucking believe it?" Yes I would: I alone know your destiny.

And now the year is coming to a close and I can feel my noble, giant of a husband slipping away from me again. Come back to me, Billy. I'm fading away again ...

The digested read ... digested

He walks, he talks, he swears, he turns 60. Fucking amazing, Pamsy.

Broken Music

Sting

Rio 1987. It's the weekend before I'm due to play the world's biggest ever gig, and Trudie and I are being driven deep into the rainforest to partake of the sacred ayahuasca. I have momentary misgivings and picture the negative headlines. Trudie reassures me and gulps the potion. I do likewise. I feel violently sick and then my mind fills with strange hallucinations: the first world war, my mother groping another man in an alley, my father's look of hurt, my alienated childhood. And when I come to, I have just one thought. All you need is love. Deep.

* * *

This is not intended to be a straightforward autobiography. Rather it will be like my music: a series of atavistic, yet profound and moving sounds that combine to create something utterly predictable and dull.

I was born in the north-east. My father was a milkman and my mother felt constrained by the routine of their lives.

"Oi, Gordon help your mum with shopping," my father barked.

"My name's Sting."

"Next you'll be telling us you think you can sing."

"We are a family cloistered in silence," I replied smugly.

I was far more intelligent than all my friends, and their resentment fuelled my inner sense of loneliness. My search for understanding drew me further into my music, and I remember hearing the Beatles for the first time and thinking that one day they might even be nearly as influential as me.

Alone in my bedroom at home, I lovingly practised on an old acoustic guitar, until there was no tune I hadn't mastered. With my talents it was hard to know what instrument to play. I found myself drawn to the more understated, yet more complex, demands of the bass.

My accomplishments rapidly brought me to the attention of all the musicians at the Newcastle YMCA and I played in a series of bands in the early 70s that didn't get the credit they deserved.

Naturally there were many women drawn to my presence – Megan and Deborah to name two – but it was the actress Frances Tomelty I chose to bless with marriage. Until I was famous, of course, when I left her for Trudie. But Trudie did look exactly like Deborah, who had died, so there was a cosmic reason for us coming together.

I was eventually invited down to London to practise with a drummer called Stewart Copeland. He was extremely impressed with me, though he was later rather annoyed that our first album contained many more of my songs than his. As the Police we became the most famous band in the world, and then I split it up, as I had always known I would, because I needed to do my own thing. And for no good reason I'm going to stop here.

The digested read ... digested

The Tantric autobiography – goes on way too long and is only of interest to the writer.

Are You Talking to Me?

John Walsh

It all began when I awoke feeling breathless at 3am – the kind of feeling every literary man nearing 50 gets when he's due to have lunch with his publisher and he hasn't got an idea to pitch.

I looked around the room; it was dark apart from the amber glow of the light on my computer. Through a gap in the curtains, I could just make out a few stars. And then it hit me: I had subconsciously arranged my room to look like the film set of *2001: A Space Odyssey* without even realising it.

Here was the big idea. I'd seen quite a few movies in my life, so surely I could get away with refracting my life through the prism of the silver screen – I'd done exactly the same thing for my Oirishness, so why not for film? But where to start?

How about with *Mutiny on the Bounty*? Even as a nine-year-old boy in 1962, I sensed that the world order was about to collapse. Where others may have just seen an adventure movie, this film spoke to me of a complex Hegelian dialectic – of the way power structures were now free to be subverted.

Unlike many boys, I immersed myself in the Western genre. I wanted to be John Wayne. We had so much in common. Like the name John. No longer would I be terrorised on the bad streets of Battersea by local youths. "Come on punks," I would say. "Make my day." Or was that another film?

My friend Chris told me *The Sound of Music* was all about the awakening of adolescent sexuality. "All you've got to do is whisper, I am 16 going on 17," he confided, "and you're guaranteed a snog." I have to say it never worked for me then and it hasn't worked for me since. Not even in the Groucho club at 2am. Still, that's another chapter out of the way.

Bonnie and Clyde heralded a new era of filmic amorality, and Clyde had the most fantastic waistcoats. I saved up for an outrageous gold shirt which some people found quite cool. Oh dear. This is beginning to look a bit thin, isn't it?

I suppose I ought to mention a few foreign films now. There isn't much to tie them into my life, but it will look clever. So here goes: *The Enigma of Kaspar Hauser*, *La Strada*, *L'Année Dernière à Marienbad*. That should do.

By 1973, I had a girlfriend, Juliet, whom I took to see *Don't Look Now.* Watching the film, I felt my life unfolding before me. Had I not had two parents? Had I not nearly drowned once? Had I not been to Venice? "This is the most important film ever made," I said to her grandly.

"It seems like a pretentious Hammer film with clever editing," she replied.

But she was wrong. It was much, much more than that. Above all, it was the ending for my book.

The digested read ... digested

Of all the books in all the bookshops in all the world ... this one had to land on my desk.

How to Lose Friends and Alienate People

Toby Young

It wasn't fair. Julie Burchill wouldn't play magazines any more.
So I went off to New York to be important.

"Wow, Graydon, baby, cool office you've got." I flicked some
ash from my 501s, and leant across the huge mahogany desk
of the editor of *Vanity Fair*. "Stick with me and we'll make
something of your shitty little mag."

"Youfuckinsonofabitch."

"Relax man," I whispered. "It's just cool British irony."

"Go back to your cupboard and write some captions," Graydon
barked.

"Cor, look at the threepennies on her," I said to Elizabeth, leafing
through some stills in the fashion editor's in-tray. "Have you
any idea why I can't get laid?"

"Where shall I start?"

"Don't you just hate all these jumped up celebs?" I continued.
"Could you get me in to the opening of the nearest fridge? Please.
PLEASE."

"You're a fucking crap writer, you know, Graydon," I said,
cleverly. "How come you're giving me so little work?"

"Oh, get out of my hair and go and interview someone."

"How about Martin Amis?"

"Go fuck yourself," said Mart.

"Look, Toby," levelled Graydon, "you can interview Nathan
Lane. He's a nice boy. You can't fuck that up."

"So, Nathan," I asked, subtly, "is it true you're a Jewish pooftah?"

"I'm really sorry about Nathan, Graydon," I grovelled. "But I've got a surefire proposal. How about I do something on Cool Britannia?"

"Nice one, Tobe. We'll get someone else to write it, though. You can go along as a photographic assistant. You can't fuck that up."

"Is four grams of coke enough, Damien?" My efforts to brown nose the king of BritArt were futile.

"Congratulations," sneered Graydon. "You did fuck it up. You're fired."

"No, honestly, Graydy," I pleaded. "I've got some great new ideas. How about I upset those sycophantic phonies Harold and Tina?"

"You're fired."

I mooched alone in New York. No job, no prospects, no shag, no hair. Then suddenly, Caroline, the fairy princess, came to the rescue.

"You shall come to the ball," she said, "and you shall write a book and be the talk of *le tout Londres*."

The digested read ... digested

He came, he saw, he failed.

Dear diary

The Letters of Kingsley Amis

edited by Zachary Leader

My dear Philip,

So very sorry not to have written earlier, so very sorry. I haven't done much of anything since my wife left me. Not for anyone, she just buggered off. I think she did it partly to punish me for stopping wanting to fuck her and partly because she realised I didn't like her any more. Even so, not having her around is infinitely crappier than having her around. I did feel better for 20min today, though, as I have just found and installed the couple who will look after me. They are Hilly and her third husband, Lord Kilmarnock.

I'm still working on the Welsh novel, *Iv dn bggrll*. I'm so painfully slow. I have to keep checking the Welsh dictionary, and have come up with the not particularly Taffy suggestion that the reason women live longer than men is that a good number of women knock off their husbands with rage-induced coronaries. What do you think?

I saw your piece on Waugh. It sounded a fucking dreary book. The more I think about it the more I reckon he wrote one good book and then went off when he became a Catholic. The thing that really gets me about him is the way he toadies to the upper classes, droning on and on about how wonderful everything about them is. Still, he isn't as bad as Bron, I suppose.

Bin reading the new Tony P. It starts OK but then falls apart. Pissy as it is, though, it's not half as bad as the bunch of new books by the leading young novelists I've been sent. Not that I've read them all. As if. One William Boyd short story goes on and on, and just when you think something is about to happen it ends.

And then there's M**t** *m*s. Don't know what to say about him, though I bet you do. He made £38,000 last year. The shit. The little shit.

NB: Have you read the new Dick Francis? He's back to form with *The Danger*. I went out to lunch with the Penguin publicity girl yesterday and quite enjoyed it. It would have been bloody brilliant if I had actually wanted to fuck her. It wasn't her fault. My sex drive just isn't what it was.

My damn fool doctor has told me I ought to give up the booze as I've been getting spasms in my arm. But what's left if you can't drink? So sod him. I am on my New Alcoholic Policy of four to five drinks per day. It allows me to eat, sign my name and follow films on TV. But it doesn't stop the nightmares. I'm piling on the pounds. I now have a 42-inch waist rather than the normal 38. Growing old is hell. What a feast future generations will have when they read our letters.

Happy and prosperous new bum,

Kingers

The digested read ... digested

Grand old curmudgeon turns out to be consistently more entertaining as a letter writer than as a novelist. Did I tell you about that girl I met? Pass us a drink.

Alan Clark

The Last Diaries

Saltwood/Albany, February 1991 – September 1999

Still obsessive about "X" but haven't the nerve to end it. Darling Jane is looking strained, she knows something is up. Tension headache; my pulse up to 87. I'm not at all well. How much longer have I got? Five years? Ten years. Finances in a total mess. Don't want to get rid of Big Red so might have to sell the Degas; 300 would clear the tax bill. State of abject depression. The party is in a mess and I feel now is the time to step down. But I can't bring myself to do it yet as ACHAB.*

Slept very badly. Had to get up three times for a tinkle. I must book a PSA. "X" is ignoring me and I'm taking it out on Janey. Cleared my office at Westminster and said my goodbyes; my health is good, my stamina is up but my mood is black. I SHOULD NEVER HAVE LEFT THE HOUSE OF COMMONS. I really need to organise a car cull and get on with my life. God has been good to me; I've had a great career, sex-life with Janey has never been better and there's the prospect of grandchildren on the horizon.

Is it too much to ask for one last chance at power and 10 more years? Richard Ryder isn't returning my calls – little shit. How I miss the thrill of power. JM is almost isolated, the party rudderless. Publication of my diaries has caused something of a stir. It's nice to still be famous. Or should that be infamous?

Desperate to get back into the House. Had an approach from Kensington & Chelsea but Nick Scott is hanging on. Am I too old? Still, ACHAB. My vision is going. Cancer of the optic nerve? Scott inquiry still rumbles on, find it increasingly hard to trust

Tristan G-J. See in the *Sunday Times* my name has been put forward as possible leader of the Tory party. I feel marvellously young once more. A miracle. K&C have adopted me against all the odds. But how long will I be alive to enjoy it? Disastrous general election, but my seat quite safe.

Alastair Campbell phoned twice to offer me a K. BB published but poor reviews. My headaches are getting worse. The doctors say there is nothing wrong with me.

The fact is I have a brain tumour and I'm going to die.

*Anything can happen at backgammon.

The digested read ... digested

AC's observations on both his health and his fellow politicians remain spot on to the last.

The Smoking Diaries

Simon Gray

Here I am, two hours into my 65th year, farting, belching, dribbling and ... where was I? Ah yes, wheezing. You might say: "What do you expect if you continue to smoke 65 cigarettes a day?" I won't mind if you do; it's a conversation I have each day with myself. I hate being this old, this debilitated and it's a sad truth that I'm a great deal nastier than I was ... oh, a year ago.

The doorbell rang this evening, but neither Vic nor I could be bothered to answer it as we assumed it was burglars. We later ran into Harold and Antonia in the restaurant and Harold told us he's got cancer of the oesophagus. First Ian, now Harold. At least Harold's still alive. It wasn't meant to be this way: it was always our assumption that I'd die first. I almost made it a few years back when my liver collapsed under the effects of years of hard drinking. But I came back from the dead and ... well, I'm still here.

The only writer who ever made a real difference to me was Hank Janson. In the early 1950s he wrote what would now be called erotic thrillers. My brother Nigel and I kept a goodly selection, though I suspect I was rather more fervid in my enthusiasm for the Janson oeuvre. Mummy was careful to leave me to him: but then our family was always careful to leave distances between each other. It was Granny who told me that Mummy had flown home to London to be with Father, leaving us boys to see out the war in Canada. I wonder if she knew about Father's affairs?

It's raining here in Barbados. I watch a woman prepare a lounger for her husband, who clearly suffers from Alzheimer's.

Vic and I met them this evening. It turns out the old man doesn't have Alzheimer's. Strange. I preferred him when I thought he did.

My mother died of cancer when she was 58. Before she died, she told me: "Si, I've learned my lesson. I'm never going to have another cigarette." Father never learnt his. He died in the same ward, pining for a cigarette. I've just been told I've got prostate cancer. That squares the circle with Ian and Harold. "We're not going to treat you," the doctor said. "There's so much wrong with you, something else will kill you before the prostate." I'm not sure whether to be worried or reassured. I'll have a cigarette and think about it.

I love the Italian coast, but this trip brings back painful memories. When I had money and was successful, I lived like a king. Now I'm in the Hotel Metropole. What happened to my prosperous self? It vanished, I suppose, with some help from me. What little I hadn't spent, I invested in Lloyd's.

I've tried explaining to Vic that I'm ill, possibly very ill. She nods and continues packing. I look through an old photograph album. I recognise the pictures of Nigel, Piers and Mummy. But I look at myself and think: who is this?

The digested read ... digested

Postcards from the last gasp saloon.

Primo Time

Anthony Sher

2 November 2002: I wonder if Nelson Mandela knows Primo Levi. I'm on my way to meet Nelson and I'm planning to adapt Primo's *If This Is A Man* as a one-man show; it would be a remarkable coincidence if there was a tangible connection between three of the most iconic figures of the 20th century.

7 November 2002: At Grayshott health farm with my dear friend Richard Wilson. I mention the project to him and he replies, "But of course you must play Primo." I immediately see he's right.

8 November 2002: Sod it. I start writing tonight.

9 November 2002: Finished. It's far too long, but I could sense Primo's presence guiding me. I am wrung out I have cried so many tears.

27 November 2002: Dearest Greg says it's the best thing I have ever written. Richard, too, has been terribly affected by the script and has agreed to direct me.

10 January 2003: I am bereft. Nick Hytner has said he's not sure Primo is right for the National and my agent says Primo's estate is extremely reluctant to give permission for his work to be adapted for the stage. Don't they understand Primo is not just theirs? He belongs to the world. How many more bitter tears do I have to weep?

20 July-18 October 2003: I am doing *I.D.* at the Almeida and The Fear is gripping me. Will I walk off stage? No.

5 January-17 July 2004: The six months of *Othello* are far too big a story to tell here. I will publish my diaries on this later.

18 July 2004: Rehearsals start today. The Levi estate adore my script and Nick H promised me the Cottesloe, yet I feel flat. Is The Fear returning?

27 July 2004: Richard has suggested some punishment exercises to try to access Primo's psyche within the concentration camp. I am deeply apprehensive.

30 July 2004: I haven't been able to write about myself for several days. Richard forbade it. That was my punishment. It may not be quite the same as Auschwitz, but I have been shaking with terror. I can almost sense Primo talking to me.

18 August 2004: First costume fitting and my shoes from Harrods are perfect. Richard wants me to be more restrained. It feels strange not to over-emote.

23 August 2004: The day started badly with Greg spilling my champagne but ended well after a session with my therapist. We were talking about The Fear when I said, "It wasn't Auschwitz that made Primo commit suicide: it was his depression." "You're so wise," she smiled.

15 September 2004: I have started writing letters to Primo. Dear Primo, I hope you like my play. Love, Tony.

29 September 2004: A red light came on in the dress rehearsal. How can I work with such distractions?

30 September 2004: The first night. Everyone thinks I'm marvellous. If only Primo would write back to me ...

The digested read ... digested

If This Is an Actor.

The Diaries of Kenneth Tynan

edited by John Lahr

June 1971: Chronically idle since my return from France. I used to take Dexamyl to give me confidence to start work. Now I take it to give me the confidence not to.

April 1972: I talk to John Dexter and Frank Dunlop about LO's willingness to sell us all at the National to P Hall. Hall is one of those curious types with no enemies and no friends.

October 1972; One difference between the London theatre today and 20 years ago is the relative paucity of queers.

February 1973: I have been seeing a fellow spanking addict, an actress called Nicole. Her fantasy is to be bent over with knickers down and caned, preferably with the buttocks parted to disclose the anus. She also enjoys spanking and exposing me. Really there is no sport to touch it; it is not just a nocturnal relaxation, it is a way of life.

April 1973: My birthday. Noel is dead and Muhammad Ali has broken his jaw and I am 46. God and bugger and fuck.

September 1973: For lunch and dinner at Tony Richardson's villa near St Tropez. John Gielgud asks me about *The Joint* by James Blake. KT: It's about a masochistic convict who gets himself imprisoned because he likes being sucked off by sadistic Negro murderers. JG: You can't quarrel with that.

May 1974: What is my current profession? Drama critic: not since 1963. Impresario: not since *Oh! Calcutta!* Nabob of the NT: not since last December. Film director: untested. Journalist: extinct. Author: blocked. I have no professional identity and have ceased to exist.

July 1975: General depression due to persistent bronchial infection.

March 1976: At last able after many months to make love to Kathleen again. But my potency vanishes after she spends another night with her lover, Dan Topolski. Debts now mountainous yesterday the telephone was cut off. I can't write without smoking and if I smoke I shall die. Vicious circle or double-bind. Compare and contrast.

November 1977: A cheque for $22,000 – three times the amount agreed – arrives from the *New Yorker*. For a day I am surely the best-paid journalist in the world.

January 1980: Debts in excess of $75,000 and health failing rapidly. From Maugham's *The Summing Up*: He leaves out his redeeming qualities and so appears only weak, unprincipled and vicious. Shall I fall into this trap?

The digested read ... digested

High angst, top gossip and lashings of S&M from the final years of one of Britain's most talented theatre critics.

The Journals of Woodrow Wyatt:
from Major to Blair, 1992-97

Everyone has been congratulating me on being the only person to predict the outcome of the election. Except Rupert, who was a little short with me on the phone. I hope I am not on the way out from *The Times* or the *News of the World*.

Have been reading the proofs of William Shawcross's biography of Rupert. I sent William a stiff letter saying how badly he had misjudged Rupert and that he wasn't an enemy of the people. I also faxed Rupert a copy of this letter without telling William. Rupert telephoned to thank me and praised me for my insight.

Have written to all the new ministers to tell them how delighted I am by their appointments. My dear friend Norman is thrilled to have been given the grace-and-favour home Dorneywood, as it signifies he is not just a short-term chancellor.

At a party at the Channon's, Bianca Jagger remembered meeting me in the House of Lords. She is very pretty and must be like an octopus to go to bed with. Apparently, it wasn't Bianca after all; still, she's posh and foreign so it was an easy mistake to make.

Andrew Morton's biography of Princess Diana has just been published, and it's full of ridiculous suggestions that Prince Charles has been having an affair with Camilla Parker-Bowles. The Queen Mother, looking as gracious as ever, thanked me for what I wrote as we sat in the Royal Box at Ascot.

Poor Margaret. Major is being so beastly not making her a Life Countess. I invited her to dinner to commiserate. "At least

Mark will be all right," she said. What a marvellously stoical woman.

Petronella wrote an article in the *Sunday Telegraph* about Margaret which said she might have got something wrong once. I must have a word with her about being snide. If she doesn't crawl no one will speak to her.

Poor Norman had to take all the flak for the ERM debacle, when he had been advising John to bail out days ago. Must put the record straight in my column.

Poor John having to deal with so many shits. England will commit an act of collective lunacy if it votes in Blair.

My throat is horribly constricted; I wonder if it is related to my chest infection.

The digested read ... digested

The Voice of Reason makes his third bid for stardom.

Thrillers

State of Fear

Michael Crichton

A scientist dies in Paris after having sex with a mysterious stranger. A supplier of mining equipment is also killed in Canada. Nobody – least of all the reader – pays any attention. Except Kenner, the MIT-educated, special-forces-trained lone wolf.

"Hmm," he smiled grimly to himself. "The environmental activists are on the move."

Back in California, Nick Drake, head of the National Environmental Resource Fund (Nerf), was sharing his thoughts with George Morton, his tycoon backer.

"It's really heavy," said Drake. "The water level of the Pacific has risen so much that these islands are going to be swept away. We need money to sue the multinationals for global warming."

"You got it," replied Morton. "I love this planet."

Peter Evans, Morton's attorney, and Sarah, Morton's impossibly beautiful PA, nodded in agreement. "We love this planet."

Two weeks later, Morton appeared drunk when he got up to speak at a Nerf gala. "Global warming's a load of rubbish," he shouted, before driving off in his Ferrari.

Peter and Sarah tried to follow him, but found only his wrecked car. There was no sign of his body. "Guess he must have been thrown into the ocean," they sobbed.

"Give me Morton's money," yelled Drake.

"I can't," replied Peter. "His estate is in probate."

Drake stormed out.

"What are we going to do now?" asked Sarah.

"Not so fast," said Kenner, abseiling in through the window.

"You two are coming with me."

On the way to Antarctica, Kenner delivered a long lecture on how global warming wasn't really happening and that many scientists had allowed themselves to be lured into a state of fear by environmental pressure groups.

"Nerf is funding terrorists to create environmental catastrophes to reinforce their message," warned Kenner. "We have to stop them."

A day later, Sarah and Peter crawled out of a crevasse. They were bruised and bloodied, but at least they had prevented a huge piece of the ice-shelf from being carved off into the ocean.

Two days after that, Sarah and Peter crawled out of a mudslide in Arizona. They were bruised and bloodied, but at least they had prevented another disaster.

"Just the Solomon Islands to go," yelled Drake.

Sarah and Peter looked at each other. They were about to die trying to save the world from a tsunami and they hadn't declared their love for one another.

"I'm alive," shouted Morton, as he rescued them. "The world is saved, and I'm going to start a new environmental organisation based on truth."

Author's note: I'm very, very clever and have read a lot and you're all stupid wishy-washy liberals.

The digested read ... digested

In the beginning was the Word, and the Word was with Crichton, and the Word was Crichton.

The King of Torts

John Grisham

Clay Carter sat down next to his fiancee, Rebecca, in the lounge of the Potomac country club.

"So, loser," leered her father, "why don't you come and work for a friend of mine and earn some proper money?"

"Because I like working in the Office of the Public Defender," he squealed. "It's noble, right and American to defend crackheads like Tequila Watson."

"Oh, Clay," cried Rebecca, "I'm going to have to call off our wedding."

The very next day a mysterious man walked into Clay's office. "Forget about Tequila," he said. "The reason he did what he did was because the pharmaceutical company hadn't tested his Tarvan properly. So sue the company instead. Here's how you do it."

Clay felt a little bad about abandoning his principles, but the Porsche and the expensive town house looked good and he had cut some of his colleagues into his good fortune.

The class action against Tarvan worked a treat, and Clay enjoyed the feeling of $15m in his back pocket.

The mysterious man appeared again at Clay's office. "I've got the lowdown on another drug, Dyloft," he said. Clay ran some ads and signed the clients. This time he did a bit of insider dealing on the share price, made another $100m and bought himself a jet.

"Wow, you're the king of torts," shouted all the other lawyers.

Clay felt a bit sorry for himself when he saw that Rebecca was getting married. "Find me a girlfriend," he barked to Jonah.

"How about Ridley?" Jonah said. "She's a Latvian pole-dancer."

"Sounds classy. She'll look good in my villa in the Bahamas."

The mysterious man appeared again. "I've got another drug, Maxatil."

Clay signed the clients but the other lawyers weren't so impressed. "I'm not sure you'll win this one," they said. A little while later Clay discovered the effects of Dyloft were more severe than expected and that he had ripped off his clients.

"I'm a bad, bad man," he wailed. "I have followed the path of materialism and abandoned the path of righteousness. I have made innocent people suffer."

The Maxatil case collapsed and Clay went bankrupt. "Oh, Rebecca," he sighed, "leave your husband and let's just live on love and goodness and air."

"Oh, Clay," she swooned with gratifying gravitas.

The digested read ... digested

Dizzyingly complex morality tale from the man who earns a fortune churning out pap.

Pompeii

Robert Harris

"Aquarius, come quick!"

Marius Attilius stopped work on the Aqueduct Augusta, which provided water to the seaside resorts of Pompeii and Herculaneum.

"Please, Aquarius," cried the girl. "My father is putting a slave to death for something he hasn't done."

Attilius followed the girl, Corelia, to the luxury villa of her father, Ampliatus.

"Your negligence has killed my prize fish," Ampliatus said to his slave. "I shall throw you to my moray eel."

"It's not his fault," yelled Attilius. "There's sulphur in the water."

But the slave was dead.

It had only been two weeks since Exomnius had disappeared and Attilius had taken command of the water supply, but already he was sickened by the decadence all around him. Had he been alive nearly 2,000 years later it would surely have reminded him of life under Georgius Bushius Americanus and Donaldus Rumsfeldus Maximus.

Attilius's heart skipped a beat. The water was not flowing in Neapolis or Misenum. He rushed to Admiral Pliny.

"Please lend me a boat so I can go to Pompeii to mend the aqueduct."

Pliny shifted his vast bulk and consulted one of his learned tomes.

"I trust you, Aquarius."

Attilius did not trust either Corax or Bebix. But he needed their help to fix the blockage.

The boat pulled into Pompeii, and Attilius knocked on Ampliatus's door.

"I need men and oxen."

"You shall have them. Can I bribe you with anything?"

"I am incorruptible."

"Then you must die," he whispered.

"Oh what shall I do?" cried Corelia. "My father is planning to kill Attilius. I must let him know."

Attilius found the blockage on the side of Vesuvius. It was unlike anything he had ever seen before. The concrete appeared to have lifted and it took a superhuman effort to get the water flowing.

Corelia appeared. "My father used to bribe Exomnius to supply him water on the cheap. Your purity has signed your death warrant."

Corax approached Attilius with murderous intent. Just as he was about to strike, he slipped into the molten ash of the volcano and died.

"What an anticlimax," said Attilius and Corelia.

"Exomnius knew Vesuvius was due to blow," cried Attilius. "I must warn Pliny."

"I have written many books on volcanos," said Pliny. "I must see this for myself."

"We must escape," shouted the sailors as pumice rained down on Stabiae.

"I want to die here," Pliny replied nobly.

"I must go back to Pompeii to save Corelia," said Attilius.

"I will stay here with all my money," Ampliatus cried defiantly.

Attilius picked up Corelia and carried her in his arms.

"Come with me up the hill and hide in the aqueduct."

And they both lived happily ever after.

The digested read ... digested

Not with a bang but a whimper.

Absolute Friends

John le Carré

Who is this Ted Mundy scratching out a living as a tour guide in one of Mad King Ludwig's castles? See how he peppers his spiel with asides about Bush and Blair's imperialist war. He pretends not to notice a face. Oh yes, sir, he is a professional. He waits till the room empties before examining the note. What can Sasha want?

* * *

See young Ted, growing up alone in Pakistan. His father is a drunk; he does not know his mother was an Irish maid. How early the deception starts. Oh yes, sir. He goes to boarding school in England. He feels alone but he is taught a love of Germany that stays with him.

At Oxford, he is again the outsider, but Ilse teaches him of love before rejecting him. "Go to Berlin," she says. "Tell Sasha I sent you."

Here is Ted standing by the Wall. He has joined forces with the intellectuals who have rejected their bourgeois roots. Oh yes, sir.

"Fuck off," says a voice. It is Sasha. Ted and he will soon become firm friends. Sasha is a misformed dwarf, a leader of the student revolution, whom all the women adore. "I have told no one that my father was a Nazi Lutheran minister," he confesses.

Sasha is falling under the blows of the West German riot police, before Ted carries him to safety. "You are a hero of the revolution," Sasha says.

Back in England, Ted marries Kate, who will become one of the modernisers of the Labour party. Suits you, sir. Ted starts working for the British Council, and escorts a theatre group through eastern Europe.

Ted worries that the leading lady is planning to smuggle her Polish lover back to England. What should he do?

"He's a KGB plant," whispers a voice. "The border guards will not find him, they want him to get through." Ted looks round. It is Sasha.

"I'm working for the Stasi," he continues. "It's a mistake – I did it to spite my father but he, too, is a Stasi hero. So I am going to be a double agent. You will be my contact. You must pretend to want to spy for the DDR."

Ted meets Amory, his British control, and the deal is agreed. For years Sasha passes information to the west, while Ted feeds the Stasi next to nothing. Ted's marriage ends, but he is happy in his work. Then the Wall comes down and Ted and Sasha are left rootless.

* * *

"Meet the people who want to set up a counter-university," says Sasha. "An institute free of western dogma." Ted has his reservations. The money comes from Riyadh and nothing is what it seems. Could it be an al-Qaida front?

Amory warns him it could be a CIA covert operation. Ted visits the school and he and Sasha are shot by German and US special forces. The west claims a victory in the war on terror.

The digested read ... digested

Two *Fast Show* cold war double agents come unstuck in Blairtopia.

Hard Revolution

George Pelecanos

1959: The radio broadcast another lynching down south. Derek
Strange flicked the dial – enough political context. Bo Diddley
came on. Even at 12 years old, Derek preferred a musical
namecheck to proper characterisation. But everyone did in this
part of downtown DC.

"Let's go rob the store," said Martini. Derek felt his guts churn.
But how could a black boy say no? A hand grabbed his shoulder.
"You got something, son?" the owner asked. Derek handed over
the padlock. "You done wrong, boy. But I'm gonna let you go.
Don't let me down now."

Later, Derek lay in bed listening to "The Girl Can't Help It",
wondering when Dennis, his brother, would get back.

1968: The Vietnam war was going badly, President Johnson
had just said he wouldn't seek another term, and Dr King was
due in Memphis. Derek flicked the dial, and found the R&B
AM station – enough political context. "It's tough being a black
police officer," he thought.

Buzz Stewart, Walter Hess and Martini checked out a Miracles
record on WHMC. "I prefer Wilson Pickett," snarled Stewart. He
didn't like music too niggerish. They cruised off looking for action.
"Hit that nigger," he ordered. The body crumpled under the
fender. "How many points for that monkey?" Hess laughed.

Detective Vaughn hated homicides. He didn't much like his
son's taste for Hendrix, either. "I'm gonna get the bastards who
killed that coloured," he said to Olga. "If you mean black, then
say so," she snapped.

Alvin Jones, Ken Willis and Dennis Strange had been smoking marijuana. "Ray Charles, James Brown and Gladys Knight are in town next week," wheezed Dennis. "Enough of that," said Jones. "We're gonna do that market."

Dennis wanted out. He caught a couple of lines of "Love is Here and Now You're Gone" before making a call. "There's gonna be a robbery at your store tomorrow."

The police picked up Willis outside his apartment. He had time for one coded call to Jones. "You're dead, nigger," Jones growled as he pumped a slug through Dennis's temple. The radio played, "Bye bye, love ..."

Vaughn received two calls. One from the garage mechanic, one from the store warehouse man. He had the guys who had hit and run the black boy, and was confident he had the killer of Strange's brother. "You wanna sort this out with me?" he asked Derek.

There had at last been some real action so the radio wasn't playing when news came through that Dr King had been shot. Within hours there was rioting in DC. Vaughn and Strange made their way through the crowds. "You killed my brother," said Derek. Jones ran. Derek heard two shots, then Vaughn appeared. There had been 12 riot deaths: the 13th would go unnoticed.

Derek lay back on his bed. Dylan came on the radio. The Times They Were a Changin.

The digested read ... digested

The first episode of Derek Strange's *Desert Island Discs*.

Liberation Day

Andy McNab

The sub surfaced just off the Algerian coast. "Ready?" I barked to
Hubba-Hubba and Lofti. They slung their waterproof bags over
their shoulders and nodded. We dived in and headed for the
shore. A three-mile swim in icy waters was nothing compared
to my training in the Regiment. It was then just a 20km sprint to
Zeralda's compound.

Lofti lobbed a stun grenade, and Hubba-Hubba and I ran in.
"It's a fuck-up," shouted Hubba-Hubba. Instead of just Zeralda,
there was another man, Greaseball, and a gang of frightened boys.
"Leave these pervs," I yelled. "It's Zeralda we want." I tapped him
twice in the forehead and sliced his head off.

"I swear I've given up all my dirty op work," I said to Carrie,
back in Boston.

"I know, I love you."

"That's funny," countered George, Carrie's father. "I could have
sworn you had been working for me in Algeria."

"You bastard, Nick," Carrie shouted at me. "I'm never talking
to you again."

"You bastard, George," I said.

"No hard feelings, Nick, but we need you. Your Algerian job
has put the wind up al-Qaida. You took out one of their main
hawallada, their money man, and now they are panicking. They're
sending two men to France to collect cash from their three other
hawallada. Your job is to kill them and prevent world terrorism."

"Jesus fuck, Greaseball is our contact," I said. "But we've got
a job to do, so let's do it."

Hubba-Hubba, Lofti and I recceed the marina. "I've spotted the Romeos." Lofti replied with two clicks. "Preparation is everything," I told them. "We must leave no traces." I sliced off my fingertips, burnt them and drank the ashes with a glass of my urine.

I slid on to the boat, set the charge, and followed the Romeos to the first meet. I dosed the mark with ketamine, and dumped him into the back of the Megane. One down.

"Fuck, it's a trap." Hubba-Hubba and Lofti bled to death as the lead flew.

"Don't worry," said George. "Greaseball has double-crossed al-Qaida and stolen their money. So let him go."

I thought of Hubba-Hubba and Lofti and of that pervert making off with the dosh. It wasn't enough to have prevented dozens of major terrorist incidents around the globe. I wanted revenge. I dialled the code into my phone and Greaseball's boat turned into a fireball.

The digested read ... digested

Nick Stone saves the world again and still nobody can be bothered to thank him.

Bare Bones

Kathy Reichs

Hot town. Dead baby. My brain cells fried. How was I going. To get Gideon Banks. To understand. His daughter Tamela. Had put his grandchild in a wood stove. When I only wrote. In short sentences. Except when I was going into a long scientific explanation copied from a textbook about forensic anthropology.

"Why are you called Tempe?" he asked.

"Scarpetta was already taken."

"I always knew that Tyree was no good," he added.

Back home. A swig of coke. No more hangovers. Being an alcoholic was as close as I got to having a personality.

What to pack? My first holiday in years. Could I take a chance on Ryan?

The cellphone rang. My daughter Katy. "Come to the forest tomorrow," she said. "Meet my new boyfriend."

"I'm Palmer Cousins," he smiled. "I work for Wildlife Protection." He was too cute. I didn't trust him.

Boyd skipped his lead and ran off. Frantic barks. "He's dug up some bones."

Back in the lab, I put the remains under the scope. Some bear, some human. I called Ryan. I wasn't going anywhere on holiday.

"I'll come to you," he said.

We kissed. "Down boy," I whispered.

"Me or the dog?"

"I make the gags in this book." Such as they are.

The cellphone rang. A Cessna had crashed. Suspected drug dealer.

The cellphone rang. More bones found in the privy.

The cellphone rang. Another dead drug dealer.

The cellphone rang. Two wildlife rangers had been missing for five years.

Death threats on email. I still didn't trust Cousins. He smelt wrong. The cellphone rang. A feather from a dead parrot in the bones.

Confusion. I realised that the deaths, drugs and animals were all intertwined.

It was time for the first long explanation. "The trade in animal parts is worth billions of dollars each year. It contravenes the CITES and is very wicked. Bears are chopped up for their gall bladders which are worth more than their weight in cocaine. Rare birds and plants are threatened with extinction by evil men." I looked up. Ryan was snoring.

The cellphone rang. Tyree had been found. He was working for the drug boss.

I looked at more bones. The skeleton wasn't a man, but a woman with Klinefelter's syndrome. I had located one of the agents. Almost all tied up. Cousins was going to get it.

I came round in a dark cellar. Cousins was a red herring. It was Park the coroner, who had barely featured all along. I hit him on the head as he released the snakes.

Ryan held my hand. I had been in hospital two days. "You see," I said, "Tyree and Ricky Don had a scam with galls. Aiker and Cobb were on to them. Tamela just got in the way and JJ ..." I stopped. Ryan was asleep again.

The digested read ... digested

An autopsy that does not bear forensic examination.

Very serious fiction

The Lambs of London

Peter Ackroyd

Mary Lamb ran a finger over her pitted face. Since she had been struck down with smallpox six years earlier, she had viewed herself with distaste and made a virtue of putting her brother's needs before her own. Just last night she had carried Charles to bed after he came home drunk from imbibing with his fellow clerks from the East India Company.

"Pray, listen to the opening lines of my essay for the *Westminster Review*," asked Charles. Mary sighed.

There was a knock on the door.

"My name is William Ireland," said the fresh-faced young man. "Your brother has bought a book once owned by Shakespeare from our shop, and there are still two guineas owing." Mary reached for her purse. "Say no more about it," she pleaded.

For three long weeks Mary thought of little else but William, until taking her courage in her hands she made the journey to his shop in Holborn Passage. William looked up and smiled. Truly, Mary was a lady of refinement. "Let me show you some of the papers I have recovered," he said, laying out before her a Shakespeare seal, a will that proved the bard was not a papist and his long-lost play, *Vortigern*.

"They have all been authenticated by the great Mr Malone," said William's father, Samuel. "These are verily national treasures and our shop has become a meeting place of scholars."

William held Mary by the arm. "Please take no offence," he said, "but I should be grateful for your brother's help in getting an essay published."

"It would be an honour," she replied.

Charles groaned. William had proved to be unexpectedly felicitous with words and was making quite a name for himself. "I do believe you are envious," Mary smiled.

Thomas de Quincey name-dropped his way into the story, before Richard Brinsley Sheridan arrived to declare that the Drury Lane Theatre would perform *Vortigern*.

"What thinkest thou of the poetry?" asked William. "Thou clasps thy rattling fingers to their side/And when this solemn mockery is over ..."

"'Tis fine enough," he replied. "And worthy of the bard."

The critics were divided over the play's authenticity, and William was summoned before a committee of London's finest Shakespeare scholars.

"I believe William to be an honest man," said Mary. "He has found another play, *Henry II*." Charles kept his counsel. His sister was in love, yet William's emotions were as fake as his verses.

Mary walked to Holborn to pledge her support. As she approached the shop she overheard William explain to his father how he had come to forge the papers. How could this be? She felt a tide of insanity flood over her. She ran home and stabbed her mother to death. She was later released into the care of Charles. William went on to publish 67 more books.

The digested read ... digested

From bard to verse.

Yellow Dog

Martin Amis

"I'm off out, me," he shouted to Russia.

Xan Meo looked up to see clouds like trails of spermatozoa.

"Oh God," he groaned. "I've been dumped in an ideological 1980s fictional cul-de-sac."

He strolled round Camden, thinking how far he'd come; his dad the villain, his first wife, the kids, the movie career and now *Lucozade*, his novel.

He ordered a Dickhead from the barman.

"You named him," said Mal, clubbing Xan to the ground.

* * *

"Why have I got such a ridiculous name?" groaned Clint Smoker.

"Because I say so," snapped Mart.

"So this means I'm a tabloid hack with a small cock and no girlfriend who will end up in Porn Valley and have bugger all to do with the story."

"Yep," said Mart. "But who said anything about a story?"

* * *

King Henry IX turned to his manservant. "What's all this about blekmail, Bugger?"

"We've been sent a video of Princess Victoria having lesbian sex."

"Oh dear," he eructed liverishly. "Bring me my little Chinese courtesan, He Zhezun."

* * *

"I'm goin to fuckin' do him." The accident had turned Xan into something of a satyr. "I've got to fuck you. Now," he said to Russia.

* * *

As Flight 101 Heavy fought through turbulence, Royce Traynor's coffin broke loose and crashed into the container of chemicals.

"What the fuck's going on?" said Captain Macmanaman.

"Who cares?" said the flight engineer. "We're just here as some kind of metaphor to get on the Booker shortlist."

* * *

Joseph Andrews started talking. "You know, as kids, Mick Meo and me were at each other's froats. I done him then he'd do me then we'd both do bird and ven do each other again."

* * *

"Your career's finished here, Xan," said his agent. "Go to the US and do some porno."

Hatefuck. Sidefuck. Cockout. Pornotown was a place where Mart's sexual neologisms could shine.

"So Joseph Andrews had me done cos I called someone Joseph Andrews in *Lucozade*?"

"S'right," said Mal.

"Hasn't he read any Henry Fielding? I'll do him."

* * *

"I'd never blackmail your highness; that video of the princess and He Zhezun was only insurance I'm a royalist all I effer wanted was to spend me last days back in Britain." Joseph Andrews paused the tape to gather his breath.

* * *

"I'm ready to live happily ever after now," twittered Xan.

"That's a ridiculous ending," yawned Russia.

"Well I'm bored and I've run out of ideas," said Mart.

"You said it," everyone agreed.

The digested read ... digested

Yellow Doggybollox.

Love, etc

Julian Barnes

Stuart: Hello. We've met before. Remember? I remember you.

Oliver: Oh, I remember you. How very Stuartesque. I can tell you remember me.

Gillian: You may or you may not remember me.

Stuart: Here's the story so far. Gillian and I fell in love, we got married and my best friend, Oliver, stole her off me. He hit her, I went to America, got married, became successful, got divorced (again) and came back to England where I've set up an organic veg business.

Oliver: Rush not to judgment.

Gillian: I knew Stuart was watching, so I made Oliver hit me. To drive Stuart away. It's tough for Oliver now. I'm the one with the job and the money. He's still waiting for things to happen.

Oliver: Guess who phoned last night? Narcoleptic and steatopygous Stuart. Misprise me not, I'm curious. He could also fund my scriptwriting.

Gillian: I just knew Stuart had phoned. Don't ask me how. Did I tell you that Oliver and I rarely have sex these days?

Stuart: I offered to take them out, but they couldn't afford a babysitter. Oliver patronised my choice of wine; Gillian had made a delicious lasagne.

Gillian: I'd forgotten how thoughtful Stuart is. I also burnt the lasagne.

Oliver: It all went swimmingly.

Stuart: My plan is to move them all back into a house I own. And give Oliver a job driving a van.

Gillian: It's the house Stuart and I used to live in.

Stuart: Gillian told me Oliver had a breakdown after his father died.

Gillian: Do you think I'm deliberately evading things? Oliver's become withdrawn again but the house is quite nice and the kids love it.

Oliver: Dr Robb says that part of the illness is feeling that you're never going to get better. But how do we know that voice is the illness and not reality.

Gillian: I just let Stuart slip into me.

Stuart: It was different to how it used to be. Less predictable.

Gillian: I've been protecting Stuart. He raped me. And I'm pregnant.

Oliver: Our lives are a cliche.

Stuart: Now we've had sex I'm not sure that I love Gillian as much as I thought.

Gillian: Does Stuart still love me? That's the question.

The digested read ... digested

Stuart, Oliver and Gillian still fail to relate to one another 10 years after they were introduced.

Father! Father! Burning Bright

Alan Bennett

"The hospital's just rung to say Mr Midgley's father has been taken ill," said Miss Tunstall to Mr Horsfall, explaining her interruption.

Denis Midgley, who had been having a tricky conversation about Mr Horsfall's son's hopelessness at English, realised he had just heard at second-hand his father was dying.

"You want to pray it's not his hip," said Miss Tunstall, as Midgley tried to negotiate the hospital switchboard.

"He's not at all well," said a reproachful voice. "We think he's had a stroke. It's touch and go."

"Been on the phone again, Midgley," said the headmaster.

"His father's ill. Apparently it's touch and go," mediated Miss Tunstall.

"Of course you must go," the headmaster muttered. "One's father. It's awkward, though."

Death reshuffled everything. Even the timetable. "I just never expected it," said Mr Midgley, as his wife made him some sandwiches before he left for the hospital.

"I expected it," she said, "Last time I went over, he came to the door to wave me off. He'd never done that before. It was a farewell."

"I want to be there when he goes – he loved me."

"I can't think why," countered Mrs Midgley. "It's not as if you take after him."

"I thought you'd have been here before now," said Aunt Kitty, when Midgley arrived at the bedside. "I don't dislike the oatmeal colour of the room. His doctor's black."

Midgley's father lay motionless in bed, the ghostly pallor of his

146

arms and body contrasting with the ruddiness of his face.

"I'm sorry, Dad."

Midgley waited as a man made a series of lengthy phone calls. "Could I make just one call?" he said eventually.

"Won't it wait? I'm a father."

"I'm a son. My father's dying."

"Slack tonight," said Nurse Lightfoot, the night nurse, as Midgley sat by his father's bedside through the night. "Still it just needs one drunken driver."

"What do you do all day?" Midgley asked Nurse Lightfoot the following evening as his father continued to hang on.

"Sleep."

"Maybe we could have a coffee if he's unchanged."

"OK."

"What would you say if I asked you to go to bed?" Midgley asked, as they sat on a divan in the nurse's quarters.

"I'm on an early turn."

"Tomorrow then?"

"That would be better."

The phone rang the next evening as Midgley slid his hand up Nurse Lightfoot's thigh.

"I think he's smiling," said Mrs Midgley, looking down at her father-in-law.

"Of course he's smiling," replied Midgley. "He's won. Scored in the last minute of extra time."

The digested read ... digested

Deadpan tale of sex and death in a northern hospital.

Crossing the Lines

Melvyn Bragg

The tinker drove his horse and cart through the streets of Wigton as cars hummed past. He shook his head sadly. "I'm just a cliche to illustrate how the Cumbria of the mid-50s had one foot in the past and one in the future," he thought to himself.

Sam and Ellen dwelt on the portentousness of the novel in which they were appearing. Ellen's mind turned to Mr Hawesley – she could never call him William. She knew he was attracted to her, but she could never leave Sam. These were deep, northern thoughts – the kind that were best left unarticulated.

"Our Joe's a good kid," Sam said eventually.

"Aye," Ellen replied.

Joe felt himself to be on the cusp of adulthood. He felt a longing to remain part of Wigton, yet at the same time he yearned to break free of its parochial boundaries. He sensed he had a greatness – a knighthood even – within him, but somehow it still felt an inch or two out of reach.

He stroked his thick, luxuriant hair, his enduring symbol of potency. He watched Richard swagger around the school, and felt a twinge of adolescent insecurity. Would Rachel fall for Richard's athletic charm or would his hair win the day?

"Would you like to see *On the Waterfront*?" he asked.

"Aye," Rachel answered.

"We could go dancing afterwards."

"Aye."

"So we're going out together, then?"

"Aye."

As the music changed from the foxtrot to skiffle, Joe reflected on how Wigton had one foot in the past and the other in the future.

"I'm worried about Suez," he said, a year later.

"Why are we talking about this?" Rachel asked.

"To show that this book isn't just a saga, but an important literary event that refracts global events through the prism of small-town northern life."

"I've won a scholarship to Oxford," smiled Joe. "But first I must go to Paris to be intellectual. And to show the French my hair."

Rachel lowered her eyes. She knew she was just an ordinary northern girl, and that she was losing Joe.

"Dear Joe, It's over. I've met a man called Garry," she wrote. Joe had never known such pain. "I love you," he cried. "Say we'll never be apart again."

"We'll be together for ever."

Joe tugged on his pipe and discussed Beckett with James and his fellow undergraduates. How they admired his intellect and hair. How he admired their class. He hoped Rachel would like them.

"It's over," she said. "I can hold you back no longer. Go, conquer the wider world of media and academe."

Joe knew she was right. He was too good for her. It was time to move on. But when would fame be his?

"All in good time," James muttered.

"In our time," replied Joe.

The digested read ... digested

The secret diary of Melvyn Bragg, aged 16¾.

Half in Love

Justin Cartwright

"Maybe I am a posh cunt," thought Richard McAllister, as he fingered the scar where a thug had stabbed him. "We've got a problem, minister," said Talfryn, the prime minister's press secretary. "The *Express* has discovered your affair with the actress Joanna Jermyn." Richard sighed. How dare the press contaminate the purity of his love. "There's no link between the stabbing and the affair, is there?" continued Talfryn. "Good, then the PM is right behind you."

Joanna wrapped her arms round Richard's neck. "Jeremy was a bit spiteful when I told him our marriage was over and that I was leaving him for you," she whispered. "Gosh, how I love you. Truly, madly, deeply."

Richard lay low in his brother's loft, while Joanna flew to America to make another film with Case Stipe. He tried to work on Labour's new manifesto, but politics seemed so shallow.

"The police have identified the man who stabbed you," said Talfryn. "You'll have to testify."

"I can't," replied Richard. "I didn't see him. Besides I deserved it because I'm a posh cunt."

"You have to," insisted Talfryn. "The PM's tough on law and order." "OK."

"My father's died, darling," cooed Richard. "You'll have to stay away a little longer or the funeral will turn into a circus. I love you."

How was it possible for one woman to love one man so much, wondered Joanna, as she pretended to take some coke before a meaningless actressy one-night stand with Case.

"We hear that Joanna's implicated in a drug and sex scandal," said Talfryn.

"You will still testify against the thug? Good. The PM loves you."

"It meant nothing, I love you," pleaded Joanna, but all Richard could see were the thin globules of betrayal that coated her breasts. He just couldn't bring himself to tell Joanna how much he loved her, he thought as he eased himself into Jenny, the stablehand.

"The PM is very angry that you didn't testify," said Talfryn. "Here's your resignation letter."

Richard waited at the stage door of the Almeida. "You can't come in," said a minder. "Send the limo after him," shrieked Joanna.

Richard and Joanna lay entwined, a chasm of empty promises between them.

The digested read ... digested

Richard and Joanna discover that their love for each other is every bit as narcissistic as their public personas.

The Closed Circle

Jonathan Coe

Sister dearest,

*I've come back from Italy, as things haven't worked out with Stefano.
I saw my ex, Philip, the other day, and it was strange meeting up
with Patrick after so long. He's 15 now. I'm going to stop writing to you
now, Miriam: you never write back. But you've been missing for 20
years.*

Love, Claire

It had never seemed odd to Benjamin Trotter that a pretty 20-
year-old girl should spend so much time with a nerdy 45-year-
old man. "Malvina's fascinated by my 2,000-page unpublished
novel," he thought, as he said goodbye to his wife, Emily.

By the end of the evening, he knew he had lost Malvina forever
to Paul, his brother.

"Oh Paul, you're a stunningly handsome New Labour MP,"
Malvina had said.

"Oh Malvina, you're a wonderfully intuitive woman," Paul had
replied. "You must become my PR and get me on *Have I Got News
For You*, but we must never have an affair as that would be a
betrayal of my wife, Susan."

Doug Anderton knew Paul from school. He had been an
opportunistic, shallow prat, so his meteoric rise shouldn't have
been a surprise. Still, now Doug was a top journalist he could do
something about it. "End your relationship with Malvina or I'll
expose you," he said. "And say something about the BMW sell-
off of Rover."

"We've got to end it," Paul told Malvina. Then he rang the BBC to say he was sorry about the redundancies but the market was paramount.

Three years had passed and Benjamin drove back from his meeting with Claire elated. She had always fancied him, he realised. But he had always loved Cicely, whom he hadn't seen for 25 years. How could he tell Emily?

Claire felt a sense of closure. She had uncovered her sister's murderer, but had no desire to inform the police. Instead, she would go back to Italy and live with Cicely.

Paul was astonished to see Malvina at the *GQ* party. "I've got to have you," they whispered to one another. Their lust was consummated, but Paul was a troubled man. The situation in Iraq was the first time he had disagreed with Tony, but he had voted with the government to allow him more time with Malvina. "I must resign and live with you forever," he said.

Philip and Patrick were in Berlin with Benjamin's sister, Lois, and her daughter Sophie. It was the first time Lois had been abroad since her former boyfriend had been killed in the Birmingham bombing. "After Benjamin left Emily to become a monk, he met up with Cicely again. She's now got MS and they're living together. It also turns out Malvina is their daughter."

"What a load of bollocks," Phil muttered. He noticed Patrick and Sophie holding hands. "Do you think they'll make the same mistakes as us?"

"God forbid," everyone gasped.

The digested read ... digested

All the fluff of a New Labour election promise.

The Lucky Ones

Rachel Cusk

"Your waters have broken," said Michelle.

Kirsty wasn't going to let go of the baby. They weren't going to have it. Because she came from the Barrows everyone had assumed she was guilty. But she hadn't killed Julie and the kids. Even her brief, Victor Porter, had given up on her. Last time he had sent his junior along. All she said was there was no room on the mother and baby unit and they would take the baby away.

"It's coming," she yelled.

* * *

Jane and Thomas, Lucy and Christian, and Martin and Josephine were all taking a skiing break together.

"Gosh," said Jane. "I'm so glad I'm not working for Porter any more. We might even have kids in a couple of years, won't we, Tom?"

Martin thought about Dominique and the baby back home. Was it wrong for him to feel so repelled by its neediness?

"You know, Martin," confided Christian, "Lucy doesn't really fancy me since she had the twins. I quite fancy Josephine, though."

"I'm never going to have babies," said Josephine.

* * *

Life hadn't worked out as I expected. I split up with a man I didn't love, and then I met Robert, who already had a son, Joseph, whom he loved more than me.

About this time my twin sister, Lucy, was obsessed with Serena Porter, who wrote a weekly column about how she and her children were coping with her husband dying of cancer.

"Maybe we should have had children," Robert said.

"I always wanted more children," my mother wept, "only I couldn't have any more after you were born."

* * *

"Fancy calling it Juno," muttered Mrs Daley after seeing Josephine and the new baby. "And isn't breastfeeding disgusting?"

"Mmm," replied Mr Daley, in a noncommittal way.

"I just can't cope with the baby, and I want to leave Roger," cried Josephine, as she arrived unexpectedly at her parents'.

"You're depressed," said Roger. "Having a baby brings up difficult feelings."

"Do you think the Porters will come to the drinks party?"

"Help," shouted Colin. "We've had an accident and Vanessa is hurt."

"I'm off," said Mr Daley.

* * *

Vanessa watched Colin dress and leave. He didn't want much to do with her and the boys. But she was happy, especially as she had befriended the Porters.

"We've run out of money and I'm leaving you for Lorraine," Colin announced.

Colin was a changed man after the accident. He spent more time with the kids. Vanessa was changed, too. With Victor dead, she thought she'd visit Kirsty.

The digested read ... digested

Five short stories tenuously linked by a bunch of navel-gazing baby bores.

Voyage to the End of the Room

Tibor Fischer

Here's how I became rich. I slagged off other writers and got loads of publicity. No, seriously, I stayed in on a Friday. The cheques have been coming in ever since. I have a large flat and plenty of money. When I want to go abroad I go downstairs. Tonight I am going to Finland.

London is dangerous. I don't know why nobody has thought of having more policemen. I'm sorry about these solipsistic observations but I really don't have a personality of my own, so the best I can come up with is a series of dreary aperçus Tibor has been saving up.

I bet you haven't got it yet. I don't go out at all. I didn't really go to Finland, I just own the flat downstairs and friends come over and pretend. What an amazing literary conceit! Oh, you did get it. How long ago? Surely it wasn't that obvious.

I've got a letter from Walter. He died 10 years ago. Could something be about to happen? I'll ask Audley the debt collector to find out.

* * *

I once took a job working in a live sex club in Barcelona. "Do you think you'll be able to manage it, Oceane?" asked Jorge. "Yes," I replied. Life's full of dull inconsequential conversations like that, don't you think?

Rutger always reads the same newspaper over and over again to remind himself that nothing ever happens. Does anything ever happen in your books, Tibor? "How would I know?" he replied, "I'm only up to page 116."

Walter ignores me and Heidi has just made a police helicopter crash by looking at it. Hamish is lying dead at the bottom of the pool. Merv's been shot. Moany Patricia's just died in the pool. Now Monica. Guess what? Jorge filled in the pool and a Friesian cow landed on his head. I expect you're wondering what the connections are. I am, too, because there aren't any. It's just wacky.

No one cared when I left Barcelona. I missed my flight because I wanted one last fuck with Juan and when I got to the airport I found the plane had crashed. That sort of thing happens to me the whole time.

* * *

"I signed up as a mercenary in Yugoslavia and I was about to be shot by Roberto when my mum turned up. War is a disappointment," said Audley. "What's this got to do with anything?" I asked. "Ask Tibor," he shrugged.

* * *

"I've been ripped off and Bruno still won't give me Walter's letter," moaned Audley. "It's the last time I go to Micronesia for you."

"Never mind," I answered. "You look good on webcam."

* * *

I've just heard from Walter. The letter was his way of trying to get me out the house. "Roberto's going to kill me," Audley wailed. I'd better leave the house, then.

The digested read ... digested

I am very deep.

Extremely Loud and Incredibly Close

Jonathan Safran Foer

What about a teakettle? What about little microphones? What about writing the same book again and seeing if anyone notices?

I'm nine years old and I'm an inventor, computer consultant, astronomer, historian, lepidopterist, and I write to Stephen Hawking. I'm no ordinary boy, but the creation of a writer who's trying too hard. That's why you'll find doodles, photographs, pages with just a few words on them, blank pages and very small print littered throughout the text.

Dad got killed on 9/11. We used to look for mistakes in the *New York Times* together. I picked up the messages he sent from the World Trade Center before he died, but I never told Mum. She spends most of her time with Ron.

Why I'm not where you are - 5/21/63. I've lost the power of speech, I can only communicate in writing. Then you came along, you whose eyesight was failing and asked me to marry you.

I can feel my prose dazzling from within. I find a key on the bottom of my dad's vase. This is the key to his life. I see the word "black" printed beside it and decide to visit every person called Black in the telephone directory. I will travel the five boroughs on foot and find the entrance to the mystical sixth.

My feelings - Dear Oskar, This is hard to write. Your grandfather could not speak and I could barely see, but we joined our lives in a place of Nothing and Something. He left when I was pregnant with your father. Love, Grandma.

In the evenings, I've been playing Yorick in *Hamlet*, but Mum only came once because she was out with Ron. In the day I've been walking the streets with a 103-year-old man.

Why I'm not where you are - I lost my love and punctuation in the firestorm of Dresden your grandma was her sister when she got pregnant I had to leave rather than love I wrote to my son everyday but never sent the letters I came back! to New York when I discovered he had died and went to live with your grandma again but you only know me as the Renter what is the sum of my life 4663890283648596907074645325 37

The key belongs to someone else. It has no catharsis; in its place there is only sentimentality. My mum loves me after all. My grandpa and I dig up my dad's empty coffin and we place his letters inside. I rewind the pictures of 9/11 and my dad returns to me.

The digested read ... digested

Extremely annoying and incredibly pretentious.

Spies

Michael Frayn

There it is again, the same sweet smell of privet. Now all kinds of things come back to me. Everything is as it was, yet everything is changed. It is 50 years since I was last here at the Close. There are the Averys and there is Trewinnick, home to the Juice. And is that Stephen Wheatley playing with his friend Keith?

I was always aware of my fortune in having Keith as my friend. We wore the same S-belts to schools, but his are the colours of the local preparatory school while mine are for the wrong school. I am the other ranks to his officer class.

It was Keith who found the crashed German aircraft and the apeman running amok on the golf course. And it was Keith who changed everything when he announced that his mother was a German spy. How do I feel? Envious that it is not my mother, and yet privileged that he confided in me. The Haywards had nothing to do with any other families in the Close, apart from Keith's Aunty Dee and Uncle Pete, who was away serving in the RAF.

As we began to follow her movements, it began to make sense that she should be a spy. Did I not detect falsity when she poured the lemon barley water? And when we searched her diary what were those mysterious monthly Xs?

We retired to our hideout in the bushes to keep watch. We watched her go to Aunty Dee's and disappear several times. This wasn't a ghost story, but something infinitely more frightening. She was going through the narrow tunnel under the railway into the dense woodland.

Keith and I found the padlocked tin with 20 Craven A inside, and spied his mother entering a disused underground cellar. We heard an old tramp's cough as we banged on the roof.

"Was that you, Stephen?" she said sadly later. "I warned you that some things were best kept secret."

I wasn't invited to Keith's much after that, but one evening his mother asked me to take some things to the cellar. There were noises. It was me they were after, but they got the old tramp. The train sliced him in half. It was my fault.

Keith was right, though. There was a German spy. It was me; we had emigrated to Britain in 1935 and it was to Germany I returned after the war. And did I know it wasn't an old tramp, but Uncle Pete instead? Of course I did, but even after I heard him speak I still imagined him to be a German. It is time to go now; thank you for having me.

The digested read ... digested

A Proustian whiff of privet brings back disturbing wartime childhood secrets.

Lanzarote

Michel Houellebecq

Midway through December 1999, I realised New Year was going to be disastrous – again.

"How about southern Morocco?" said the travel agent. I knew Morocco a lot better than this bitch.

"I don't like Arab countries," I interrupted, before thinking back to the wetness of the Lebanese woman I'd met at a swingers' club.

"I mean," I continued, "I don't like Muslim countries."

"How about Senegal?"

It was tempting. The white man is still king there and you don't have to pay for sex.

"I'm not up for sex."

"How about Lanzarote?"

Lanzarote is almost totally devoid of interest, having been discovered by a few Norwegians back in the 50s. You don't see them any more as they die when the sun comes out. The ordinary Frenchman runs the risk of boredom here – not something that would concern the limited minds of the Brits and the Krauts.

On the minibus trip, I noticed a dull moustachioed Belgian and a pair of German dykes. I like women licking each other. The dykes were called Pam and Barbara and I watched them play in the waves. Barbara's breasts were the most pert: they were probably silicon.

"Nice tits," I said, playing with myself.

"Thanks."

I watched TV in the hotel. The Yanks were taking over the

world again. Being governed by fucking idiots is utterly disagreeable.

I didn't see Rudi the next day. He had gone to Fuerteventura.

"It was shit," he said later, as we passed several members of the Azraelian sect.

"By the way, I only live in Belgium," he said. "I was born in Luxembourg." A country of tax evaders.

The next day we went to the beach with the dykes. Rudi disappeared, while I serviced the two women.

"You lick almost as well as a woman," said Pam. "Maybe you could impregnate Barbara."

"I'm French," I replied. "I can do anything."

Rudi was gone when we got back and I found this letter.

"I wasn't shocked by you and the dykes. My wife and I had the odd orgy until she returned to the monstrous hordes of Islam. It's just I hate being a cop and I hate living in Belgium. I'm going to join the Azraelians."

Back home I never saw the dykes again, but I followed the Azraelians in the papers – especially when the child abuse scandal broke in Belgium. Rudi got arrested as all Belgians look like paedophiles.

Hmm, I thought, as I reached page 87. Have I been *assez* shocking? Perhaps *non*. Still, stopping here and charging a tenner should piss off almost everyone.

The digested read ... digested

Damn the Mozzers, Brits, Krauts, Yanks, Belgians and Dagos. Now, can I lick you?

The Making of Henry

Howard Jacobson

Henry believes he knows exactly when the woman in the neighbouring apartment dies. He looks around his own sumptuous flat and still can't quite believe how he's come to live in this part of St John's Wood. A few months ago he received a letter telling him he had inherited the flat, but he's no idea who from. It must have belonged to his father's mistress, but he doesn't know. Or care.

He decides to go out to a cafe he's in the habit of frequenting. He orders a strudel and the smell reminds him of his father, Izzi, and his mother, Ekaterina. He remembers the shame of Izzi's affairs and his desire to protect his mother. For some reason, he also relives the sexual frisson he felt for his Aunt Marghanita. He shakes himself back to the present and leaves a pound tip for the waitress. He wonders if she notices him.

"The name's Lachlan," said the man going into the old woman's apartment. "I've waited 30 years to get my hands on this place."

Henry did not quite know what to say. Lachlan's bullying manner reminded him of "Hovis-head" Belkin, the boy who had called him a girl in his first week at school. Somehow he had remained a girl in spirit. Even at the University of the Pennine Way, where he had taught English until his retirement, he had been an honorary girl.

There were just the three of them at the funeral. Lachlan, Henry and the waitress. Henry felt a surge of jealousy. He remembered how Hovis-head always stole his girlfriends. Not that he had many girlfriends; rather he tended to borrow other men's wives for a while until they got bored and moved on. Now Lachlan had stolen his girl.

"I'm Moira," she said, flashing her thighs and revealing she was wearing no underwear. She wasn't Lachlan's girl. Henry's heart soared for the first time in 60 years. Could he be falling in love?

"It's no good," he said sadly. "Every time I try to live in the present, my mind races back to the past."

Moira could sense him drifting away again. "Look," she cried. "There's an obituary of your old-friend Hovis-head."

Henry felt a flicker of a feeling. "Thank God, he's dead," he moaned.

"Come to Eastbourne with me," Moira pleaded.

"Oh look," muttered Henry. "There's a bench with my mother's name on it. I wonder how that got there."

Lachlan raced into the apartment. "I've found the old girl's diaries. There's a reference to your mother." Henry stared in disbelief. It had been his mother who had had the affair, and left him the apartment. What's more she – a Jew – had been seeing an Arab. Somehow he could feel himself coming back to life. But still something was missing.

"I've just run over Lachlan's dog," wept Moira.

"That's it," shouted Henry. "I'm ready to live."

The digested read ... digested

A la recherche d'Henri perdu.

Finding Myself

Toby Litt

What I propose to write won't be a novel per se, rather a novelisation of events that actually happen. As I am a famous author you will pay me a great deal of money in advance. In return I will rent a house and invite some friends to stay. It will be sort of *Big Brother* meets *I'm A Celebrity* meets Virginia Woolf – it's very now and literary London will love it.

Dear Toby, it sounds terrible. I'm sure it will do well.

Why are you calling me Toby? For this book, to be called *From the Lighthouse*, I am Victoria About, the best-selling chick-lit writer.

Of course you are.

I am so excited. I've got this lovely house in Southwold – where else? – and my sister Fleur, my editor Simona and her husband William, Cleangirl and Henry and their daughter, Edith, dopey Alan, Marcia with the wheelchair, Celine, and of course my partner, X, are all staying. I've even written an outline of what I expect to happen. Obviously I'll need to do some spying, so I've set up hidden cameras in the house.

Week One: Nothing much is happening.

I'm not surprised. It was a crap idea in the first place.

You're not supposed to say that, you're my editor.

No, I'm not, I'm the reader.

How daringly postmodern.

~~Sometimes, when writing, you just have to carry on and cut the rubbish later.~~

Agreed. Though we'd better be careful, or there will be nothing left.

Help. They have discovered that I've been filming them and have locked me in the attic. And Edith says she's seen a ghost.

~~It's all going wrong: I really think I've lost control here.~~

Cut this. It was blindingly obvious this would happen from page one.

I've just discovered that people have been staging conversations to mislead me. Still, Alan and Fleur have fallen in love, so I did get something right. William has just told me he's got terminal cancer – do you think this injects a new level of pathos and reality?

Yes – Simona.

No – the reader.

I don't want to call this *From the Lighthouse* any more. Now it's *Finding Myself*.

The tabloids are on to us. Gosh, how up-to-the-minute. Oh no, X once had a gay lover. I must leave him.

~~Now I'll write five pages about the book group we held on~~ ~~To the Lighthouse.~~

Too pretentious for words.

We're only supposed to be cutting for effect, not because it really is terrible.

Tough.

It's over. X has left me, and I want him back. I don't want the book published.

It's not your call.

X has come back. Do you want to hear my new idea?

No.

The digested read ... digested

432 pages of opportunistic revelations of the bleeding obvious *aka* a masterpiece from one of *Granta's* 20 best young novelists.

The Seymour Tapes
Tim Lott

I must confess I was surprised when Samantha Seymour approached me to write the definitive version of the events surrounding her husband's strange death. My ventures into confessional writing had been limited to my book about my mother's suicide and my excruciatingly dull weekly column in a London paper.

"Why have you chosen me?" I asked, expecting her to say that only I was conceited enough to attempt to turn an obvious story about surveillance and deceit into something profound. Instead she said, "Can you be honest?"

First interview with Samantha Seymour

Why do you think Alex set up the cameras in the house?

I think he had difficulty with conflict. He thought our son Guy was stealing money, but he didn't want to make a false accusation.

Were you having an affair with Mark Pengelly?

There's no truth in this, just as there was no truth in the rumours that Alex had an affair with his receptionist.

Cyclops Surveillance Systems, first tape

You see Sherry Thomas watch Alex Seymour enter the building. He asks about installing hidden cameras in the house. There is an obvious attraction between them.

Alex Seymour's video diary

I feel so powerful. I've seen Guy steal the money and bully his sister, and I've been able to take him on. Somehow he knows I know and treats me with respect. I've also seen Sam have a smoke, despite her saying she had given up.

Second interview with Samantha Seymour

How was your relationship with Alex?

I'm not telling you unless you give me something in return.

(Author's note: I never intended to make this book about me.)

I once snogged my brother's girlfriend.

It was OK.

Sherry Thomas's flat

Sherry shows Alex a stack of videos in her bedroom. "There's one you need to watch," she says. As images of Sherry being raped as a teenager by her boyfriend's father appear on the screen, Alex masturbates. "You need to know whether Sam is being unfaithful," she says.

Alex Seymour's video diary

I now know Sam is not having an affair. I feel dirty for spying on my family. I must tell Sam everything and end the arrangement with Sherry.

Sherry Thomas's flat

Alex's body lies on the floor and Sherry inexpertly peels away the skin. (Author's note: We must presume she was searching for the real Alex inside.) She then shoots herself in the head.

Author's house

Months later Alex's children delivered a tape to me.

So you were having an affair with Mark?

Yes, I knew he was filming us and I put him off the scent.

Well, I didn't snog my brother's girlfriend, so there.

The End

I see the author. I see Sam. I see you reading the book. I see you falling asleep.

The digested read ... digested

Big Brother goes posh.

Laura Blundy

Julie Myerson

Ewan didn't like ornaments. He liked the metal dog even less when I, Laura Blundy, stove his skull in with it. I felt a soft smashing, a caving-in of bone and brain then a jet of blood sloshed out and hit the wall beneath the dado rail. I gripped my crutch tightly and caught my breath. I started laughing. A hand shot out and grabbed my ankle. He was a fighter, Ewan, I'll give him that. I picked up a poker, took aim between his eyes and pressed down, waiting for a definite juicy crunch. He didn't move again.

He had to die, did Ewan. I couldn't let anything come between me and my Billy. Billy was only 23 years old, 15 years my junior. He was a foundling, but a good husband to Cally and his kids. Ever since Billy had pulled me out of the Thames when I tried to drown myself, we had been inseparable. We loved each other, me and Billy.

Ewan never did understand why I wanted to kill myself. He was a surgeon and we had met when I was taken to hospital after being knocked down by a carriage. My leg got infected and he had to saw it off. I blacked out as he severed the membranes and grabbed the jaw-tooth saw and started working it through my marrow, turning the sawdust in the blood box into a mulch of black gruel. He had taken a fancy to me after this, and we had got married and I had tried to be the good wife, but there was so much about me I couldn't tell him.

My father had had a shop and we had been quite well-off until he died. Then I found myself on the street and I was raped when I was 15 by a gentleman in the back of a carriage and got pregnant.

I loved that boy, I really did. But living in the filth of London, with all that cess, almost killed us and I had to give him away to the Foundling Hospital.

"You've done it now, and no mistake," said Billy. We went back to the house and cut Ewan's body up. The legs and thighs came off easy, but the knife got caught in his neckbone as I tried to saw his head off. We wrapped the parts in the tarpaulin and took them to the river. We weighted the legs and chucked them in and they sank with a glorious plop. But the head, with Ewan's stupid grin taunting us, floated. We fished it out and lit a bonfire. The flesh does not burn to ashes, as you might think. It stays like charred meat and his teeth are coated shiny brown from the smoke and the fat.

"Why did you not look for your child?" says Billy. "He died," I say. "One day I went back to the hospital and was just told he had died." He asks me if I saw the grave and I tell him I never went because, and this is shameful, I went to prison. For murder. I was let out because it turned out the mother had done it, but, God knows, I had wanted to kill that baby. For being alive when mine wasn't.

We're home free, now, me and Billy. We're on the way to Folkestone to start again in France. Only I don't tell Billy that I did once go to see where he was buried. And the gravestone said, Laura Blundy. I wasn't saved by Billy, I drowned. But I have what I want. I gave you comfort once, Billy, and now I'll give it again.

The digested read ... digested

Tender gothic love story masquerading as the Victorian handsaw massacre.

Dorian

Will Self

Henry Wootton shrugged off his usual mid-morning anomie and torpidly slid a silver spike into a vein. He grunted as the barrel turned from brown to red and flushed the plunger.

"So, Baz," he sneered, "what is this new art work *de nos jours*?"

Baz Hallward looked up. "It's *Cathode Narcissus*," he remarked. "A video installation of a remarkable young man. Dorian isn't like us. He's not ashamed of being a faggot. Look at you, a sodomite married to Batface, a duke's daughter whom you treat as a convenience store."

Wootton sat transfixed as Dorian's image appeared on the screen. "I should like to meet him," he said.

Dorian picked up Herman, a rent boy, and drove round to Wootton's home. There they both helped themselves to quantities of drugs before being bandied around in a conga line of buggery. And there, too, the fatal virus began its transmission.

* * *

Wootton lay on his mattress, a barely living husk of opportunistic infections. He looked up to see Baz. "What the fuck are you doing here?" he snapped.

"I'd heard you were ill. I went to New York, introduced Dorian to Andee, and went downhill fast. I've been clean for five years, but the virus is getting to me, too."

"Get me home, I don't want to die in this place. Get me some drugs and I'll have a party."

No one had seen Dorian for years, but he still looked young, exotic, louche. Only Dorian knew the truth. He had the *Cathode*

Narcissus and he had watched the images grow old and ill.

"I've been offered a retrospective and I need the tapes," said Baz.

Baz got into Dorian's car – the last journey he would ever take. Dorian's stiletto easily dismembered the body and he carefully buried the parts.

* * *

"Well, I'm still fucking here," said Wootton. "But not for long. Tell me, did you kill Baz a couple of years ago?"

Dorian's eyes flickered. His video images had become mere cadavers.

"Everyone said you did," Wootton continued, "and that you've killed several others, too. How perfectly decadent."

* * *

Dorian read Wootton's manuscript. "How could he think all this of me?" he asked Batface. "I didn't do any of it."

He went to the urinal. "That's for Herman," spat the skinhead. Then Dorian felt the blood trickle down his neck.

The digested read ... digested

The Picture of Dorian Self.

The digested read ...

Sex; sex; sex

The Intimate Adventures of a London Call Girl

Belle de Jour

The first thing you should know is that I am a whore. Prostitution is steady work. I open my legs. And then I close them. It beats working in an office. After leaving university, I applied for a number of jobs that I never got and watched my savings steadily dwindle. So when a friend gave me the phone number of a madam, I decided to become a call girl. Like you do. And that's really all there is to me, but since I've been overpaid to write a book I'd better witter on.

Samedi, le 1 novembre. French is so sophisticated and sensual. It also reminds you that I'm middle-class and respectable, because no one's really interested in working-class or foreign prostitutes. Did I mention that I am actually rather clever? Oh, I did. Well, Martin Amis is cool.

Vendredi, le 12 decembre. My nipples are clamped and a bald-headed man is pissing on me in the bath. I knew that would get your attention.

Mardi, le 27 janvier. I have some wonderfully fascinating ex-boyfriends. Let's call them A1, A2, A3 and A4. We talk about sex all the time. A2 was telling me about his new girlfriend who is into latex. "Must be very hot," I observed.

Mercredi, le 18 fevrier. My parents wouldn't be very happy if they knew what I did for a living. I went to see them in Yorkshire last week and we went for a walk before watching *Countdown* on the television.

Mardi, le 9 mars. My publisher tells me the book needs more smut. Anal sex is the new oral. My friends have been doing it for years and I scarcely raise an eyebrow when a client asks for it.

Lundi, le 22 mars. Went shopping for lingerie with A3. I love buying knickers. Even call girls have their favourites. Had dinner with A4, and my latest lover, The Boy, walked into the same restaurant. The Boy repeatedly told me he loved me. Our relationship is over.

Jeudi, le 8 avril. I can tell you're waiting for me to say something profound. Dream on. I don't have any difficult feelings about being a prostitute. Everything's just fine. Got it? I'm just as happy fucking an ugly stranger as I am a handsome lover. The only difference is that I never come with my clients, even when I'm being fisted.

Dimanche, le 2 mai. Sometimes I lie about my age to clients. Sometimes I even lie to my friends. I guess you must be wondering whether I'm lying now.

Mercredi, le 16 juin. More smut. I always wax. The clients prefer it and it's much better for lesbian sex. A4 asked for a threesome when I mentioned this.

Samedi, le 26 juin. The madam has been giving me less work, but I don't mind because I never mind about anything. A client told me he didn't pay me for sex. He paid me to go away. I wonder if book buyers have the same attitude.

The digested read ... digested

A new variation on taking the piss.

A Round-Heeled Woman

Jane Juska

My teeth are not as sparkling as they used to be, and what was once firm is now loose. But all things considered I look good. I like men's bums and penises. At 67 years old, I am what you might call an easy lay. 'Twas not always so. In the fall of 1999 I was watching a French art house movie, when I reflected both on how little sex I'd had over the past 30 years and how unfortunate it was that I had never been published. I resolved to do something about it by placing an advert in the *New York Review of Books*.

I took my time composing the ad before settling on: *Before I turn 67 next March, I would like to have a lot of sex with a man I like. If you want to talk first, Trollope works for me.* I thought hard about mentioning Trollope as it added $30 to the cost, but I reckoned it would establish me as an intellectual and I would be more likely to sell the book. After all, no one would publish a book about geriatric sex among the lower orders.

Over the coming weeks, I received 63 replies, which I divided into yes, no and maybe. Only those from people on life-support machines or with little sense of literary appreciation made the no pile.

My first meeting in downtown San Francisco with Danny was not a success. He was rude and I told him so. My next was with Jonah, who flew in from the east coast to spend the weekend with me. He poured the champagne and I could feel myself get wet. He thrust himself inside me and I came for the first and last time. I sensed his withdrawal, his reluctance to touch me.

"What's the matter?" I asked.

"I need a paper bag."

"Why?"

"In case yours falls off."

Worst of all, he stole my champagne flutes. With two strike-outs you would have thought I might have called a halt. But, as my therapist reminded me, I had a book to write, which is why I am now going to bore you with a load of details about my family life that you can't possibly want to know.

Fifty pages later I arrived in New York to see Robert. He was old, slightly decrepit, but formidably literate. I loved him intensely, though he didn't want me and rejected physical intimacy. I took time out to see Sidney, instead.

"Take my cock," he said. I did as he asked, enjoying the power, even though his penis was slightly sub-standard.

Matt proved enigmatic, refusing to meet me, though I shall be forever grateful for his introduction to the Berg Collection. John talked dirty beautifully.

"Margaret Fuller."

"Atwood."

"Roth."

"Updike." We collapsed in a mutual orgasm on the last syllable. He then told me about his suspected liver cancer.

Graham was just in his mid-30s, though he adored Willa Cather. "I've got to have you," he said. He's arriving next week. I, meanwhile, have already arrived.

The digested read ... digested

Shagging for New England.

The Sexual Life of Catherine M

Catherine Millet

As a child I thought about numbers a great deal. What would be an acceptable number of husbands? A few, say five or six? Or many more than that, countless husbands?

I lost my virginity when I was 18, which is not especially early, but I had group sex for the first time in the weeks following my deflowering. Which may be unusual.

In the biggest orgies in which I participated there could be up to 150 people and I would deal with the sex machines of around a quarter or a fifth of them in all the available ways: in my hands and every orifice. Today I can account for 49 men whose sexual organs have penetrated mine and to whom I can attribute a name. But I cannot put a number on those that blur into anonymity.

I have grown into rather a passive woman, having no goal other than those people set for me, and I am more than dependable in the pursuit of these aims. As I was completely available, I sought no ideals in love. I was seen as someone who had no taboos and I was happy to fulfil these roles.

I was at my happiest when I was completely naked in wide open spaces, and often we would all drive down to the Bois to fuck some strangers. But confined spaces also offer a thrilling game of hide and seek. The cabs of articulated trucks suit me best, but I remember once taking refuge in the back of a Ville de Paris van and allowing the men to come in one by one. I knelt to suck them off or lay down and curled to one side the better to present my arse.

I am docile not because I like submission, but out of indifference to the uses to which we put our bodies. So I have always tried to accommodate people's preferences. The most anyone could accuse me of is a lack of conviction; one man always used to complain I wasn't good at being pissed on.

I have fucked many different types of men: old, young, tall, short, fat, slim, attractive and ugly. Appearance does not bother me too much when engaged in copulation. Fucking is an antidote to boredom. I find it easier to give my body than my heart.

The digested read ... digested

The Joylessness of Sex.

Brass

Helen Walsh

Millie: The whole of the city is aglow. I look down at the underage whore lying on the gravestone. I slip my fingers into her cunt, and slide my other hand inside my trousers. I love this feeling of the overwritten and the shocking.

Jamie: Shite. That's her on her mobie. I'm going to be late, la. I love Millie to bits. She's like me fucken sister. She's a bit posh, reet, what with her being at the Uni, but she's still a laugh. But it were better when it were just me, her, Sean and our Billy. Sean used to sell Class As. He's now got a salon an' he's given Ann Marie a job.

Millie: It's not the same with me and Jamie. I don't fancy him, like, never have, but that Ann Marie is a right bitch.

Jamie: We're driftin' apart. We all like to get eckied up, do some beak, la and hit the Stellas, but Millie, she's somethin' else. She's wastin' her fucken life. She hasn't even answered me text that me an Ann Marie are gettin' married.

Millie: What would I say? Jamie's too good for her; everyone but Jamie knows she's more than a beautician at the salon. I hit the vodka and this girl gives me the eye. "You're Professor O'Reilly's daughter. Every third-year wants to fuck him." I sober up fast. It's been me and dad ever since mum left. I can't escape this city. He needs me. I need a whore. I pay her £50 for the night. I slip a bottle inside her. I feel the orgasm of emptiness.

* * *

Millie: Herpes and gonorrhea. I can feel my cunt close down. I can feel my life close down. I'm way behind with my coursework, but I just don't care.

I call Jamie. "Let's do some E and go to Wales. Just like the old days."

Jamie: We go to Llangollen and it's almost as it was. She's loved up and me cock's stirrin' but we do nothing, cos that's not the way it is. And when we come down we're as far apart as ever.

Millie: Jamie and me are like old times. Ann Marie gave me a right look when I took him out tonight. There's this girl in the bar who's drunk and throwing up and I take some pictures of Jamie and her with her knickers down. I then take her to the toilets an' slip me fingers in her cunt. Jamie goes home an' I go off to Sean's. I've never fancied Sean. "Take me up the arse," I beg.

Jamie: Ann Marie has seen the fucken photos an' she's fucken left me. Why did you give her the photos, you bitch?

Millie: I find the letters from my mum. Why did you fuckin' hide them, Dad?

Jamie: I know it was Billy who gave the photos of me and the girl to Ann Marie. Come back, Millie, I've always loved you.

Millie: I'm off. On the bus past Glasgow. I see my mum through the window. I'm coming home.

The digested read ... digested

Where there's brass, there's muck.

Help &
self-help

The Consolations of Philosophy

Alain de Botton

I was wandering through the upper gallery of the Metropolitan Museum of Art, as one does when one has a few hours to while away before catching a London flight, when my eye was taken by a painting of the death of Socrates. "Why," I thought to myself, "has no one written a self-help book for very clever people like me?"

It wouldn't, I realised, be warmly greeted by the hoi polloi who would see such an undertaking as smug and effete, but does not Plato teach us that it's OK to be unpopular?

My mind turned to objects of desire. A neoclassical Georgian house in the centre of London; a Dassault Falcon 900C jet, stationed at Biggin Hill; the Villa Orsetti in Marlia near Lucca; a bed built into a niche in the wall (like one by Jean-François Blondel in Paris); a penthouse apartment at the tip of the Ile de la Cité (for weekends). Sadly I could only afford three of them, but does not Epicurus teach us that it is OK not to have enough money?

Even so, I sometimes feel frustrated when things don't go my way. Why is my philosophy series only being shown on Channel 4 and not on BBC1? At times like this, I turn to Seneca. Who else?

A long time ago when L and I were travelling through the Minho, I had a bad case of detumescence when we were making love. We both consoled ourselves with Montaigne's wise words on inadequacy, but I would like to reassure my female readers it has never happened again. Ever.

For some strange reason, I think of a broken heart. Imagine, if you will, a man who meets a woman on a train who reminds him of a strangely moving picture in a Danish museum. They begin to talk and she agrees to have dinner. He invites her to stay the night but she says she has to get up early the next morning to go to Frankfurt. The next day, he mopes in Battersea Park over a copy of Goethe's *The Sorrows of Young Werther*. This man is NOT me. I would have been reading Schopenhauer.

Five philosophers does not a book or TV series make. I needed a sixth. But it was difficult to think of one. In a flash of inspiration, I thought of Nietzsche, the patron saint of difficulties. Hadn't I known acute difficulties in my life? Hadn't I struggled to the summit of Piz Corvatsch, high above the Engadine valleys, to read a quote from Nietzsche that I had written on an envelope from the Hotel Edelweiss in Sils-Maria to the wind and the rocks?

The digested read ... digested

The Little Book of Calm for the chattering classes.

Packing it in the Easy Way

Allen Carr

It wasn't my ingenuity that found the only easy, pain-free way to cure people from smoking, as its discovery was one of those fortuitous once-in-a-lifetime events that just happen to you. But I do feel tremendously privileged to have helped so many people and my only regret is that I haven't yet purged the whole world of the evils of nicotine.

I was born into a poor, working-class family in south-west London. My mum never complained and my dad never talked to us and spent all his time in the pub. I can remember visiting him while he was dying from lung cancer aged 50. He made me promise to stop smoking. These were the first words he had ever uttered to me. I promised I would and promptly lit up as soon as I left the hospital, so in thrall was I to my addiction.

My life began to turn round when I passed my 11-plus and went to grammar school, as I realised education could break me free from my working-class roots. It was just a shame education couldn't release me from the cancer sticks. I passed my GCEs and got a job working for a firm of accountants. Some people say accountancy is dull, but I always found it really exciting – especially when I found an anomaly in the profit and loss account. In fact the only thing dull about me was that I had been smoking 100 Peter Stuyvesant a day since I was eight years old.

I was extremely fit and became a drill instructor during National Service, but the one thing I lacked was a girlfriend. I realised I had to become a good dancer. That I duly did and very soon after that I married Ellen. We had four children, but then we moved apart after I met Joyce, a secretary at one of the accountancy firms I worked for. Joyce was the wind beneath my wings and we soon got married.

We made a living renovating houses and the only blight on our lives was my 1,200-cigarette-a-day habit. I was literally dying on my feet. Everything changed in 1983 when I realised my nicotine intake merely replaced the insecure feelings produced by the withdrawal from the previous cigarette. I was cured forever. It was the greatest day of my life and potentially the greatest day in the history of the world.

I knew immediately I wanted to open a clinic to save everyone. Joyce was horrified when I suggested we would give a money-back guarantee if it didn't work. But I knew it would. Our first client was the radio DJ Pete Murray and shortly after that we had Derek Jameson. There have been countless other important people, such as Lord Bonham-Carter, but I am proud to treat anyone. We now have clinics in many different countries and my books have sold millions. How different my life looks after stopping smoking.

The digested read ... digested

Stopping smoking may prolong your life but it doesn't make you any more interesting.

The Universe in a Nutshell

Stephen Hawking

Apparently, a large number of the many millions who bought *A Brief History of Time* got stuck on page one. Oh dear. I expected more of my readers. With this in mind, I have now simplified some of the ideas in the hope you will make it to page two. But since you had no idea of what I was talking about first time round, this is almost certainly a total waste of time.

Still, as Einstein pointed out, there is no universal quantity called time. Instead, everyone has his or her own personal time and mine, dare I say it, is more valuable than yours. This is one of the postulates of the theory of relativity – so called because it implied that only relative motion was important.

Relativity was not compatible with Newton's law of gravity, and from this Einstein inferred that it is not space that is curved, but spacetime itself. This led us to understand that the universe is expanding. Sadly, relativity breaks down at Big Bang because it is not compatible with quantum theory. Alas, despite having worked on this problem myself, we still don't have a grand unified theory of the origin of the universe.

But back to time. Although I have my own personal time, I cannot actually say what it is. I can only describe the mathematical model for it.

The singularity theorems of Roger Penrose and myself established that spacetime is bound to the past by regions in which quantum gravity is important. So to understand the universe we need a quantum theory of gravity.

Supersymmetries provided a natural physical mechanism to cancel the infinities arising from ground-state fluctuations. This led to the discovery of supergravities and superpartners. However, in 1985, people realised there was no reason not to expect infinities and this led to one-dimensional extended object superstring theories.

But that wasn't it; Paul Townsend found there were other objects that could be extended in more than one dimension. He called them p-branes – or pea brains, as I like to call them. Ho ho. And these could be found as the solutions of the equations of supergravity theories in 10 or 11 dimensions.

Which leads us to time measured in imaginary numbers. Did you know that Richard Feynman proposed the idea of multiple histories of the universe? Just imagine it: there's even a history in which you understand this book.

The digested read ... digested

God speaks in mysterious ways.

The Shops

India Knight

What's a girl to do when she's completely run out of ideas? Write about shopping, of course!! Who could pass up the chance to witter on about their favourite shops? Not me!! I've loved shopping ever since I was five years old and I reminded my mother she had forgotten the caviar!!

Me, me, me, me!!! Fluffy, fluffy, fluffy old me!!! That's what I'll be writing about as it's the easiest way to fill space!!!! What you won't be getting is a list of boring old shops!!! Apart from on every other page!!!!! Vaishaly Patel is absolutely the place to get your brows done!!!

My mother loved shopping, my father loved shopping and I love shopping!!! Shopping is wonderful – case proved!!! People who hate shopping are just so sad!! Why don't they just get out to Fortnum's and Prada and put a smile on their faces??? Nothing gives me greater pleasure than the fact that my eldest son's two absolute most favourite foods are lobster and mussels and that my youngest son can tell the difference between Godiva and Neuhaus chocolates!!!! What better start in life could anyone in north London possibly want????

Food is absolutely the best thing in the world and there are a number of online delis – Swaddles and the Grocer on Elgin, especially – that will deliver the finest organic foods to your doorstep. I have heard there is a place called Sainsbury's that has become quite popular among the lower middle-classes, but I've never been. Can't wait to try its rack of Shropshire lamb!!!

Beauty products are absolutely the best things in the world, and some come in at less than £50 – something to suit every purse. I make no apologies for the fact that the facialist I'm going to mention is based in London. After all, I live in London and you can't expect me to find out about all the grotty beauty parlours oop north!!! Treat yourself to a day in town – Renate at Renate is more than worth the price of a day return!

Clothes are absolutely the best things in the world!! I just love the look of a man in a tapered, bespoke Turnbull & Asser shirt!!! A snip at £130, as the cuffs work in harmony with your watch!! And where would we big-bosomed girls be without Bravissimo???

Beds and chairs and kitchen things are absolutely the best things in the world. I can't understand people who settle for anything less than a £4,000 luxurious pocket-sprung VI-Spring mattress. So fluffy, and you don't want to end up deformed!! And David Champion is an absolute must for emu eggs, ornate birdcages and porcupine quills.

There's just so much to buy. Toys, flowers, pets, holidays. There's no end to the pleasure. You don't always have to go to expensive shops. My Romanian au pair tells me that Argos has some smashing things that poor people in Bucharest go crazy for. You see, shopping absolutely matters!!

The digested read ... digested

Just when you thought the chick literati couldn't get any more trivial ...

Nigella Bites

Nigella Lawson

I didn't intend to write another book so soon, but everyone was so thrilled with the sales of my previous humble efforts that they twisted my arm and it would have been churlish to refuse. Besides, I love my food and I can never resist an opportunity to witter on about it to tell the truth, I've actually put on a bit of weight recently, but this is no bad thing as it helps my women readers to realise I'm just the same as they are underneath it all.

This book will be a little different from the others. There are more pictures than before and after each chapter I've left a couple of pages blank for you to make your own notes. Feel free to doodle as you will, or to write in some of your own recipes for any of mine that don't work.

I know that many of you may not have time for the table-laden breakfast, but even the sluttiest person can whip up muffins for 12. Just make the nanny get up at 5.30am to whip up some lumpy batter, spoon it into paper cases and cook for 20 minutes. You can hop out of the bath a couple of hours later and devour them with lashings of *buerre de Normandie*. By the way, get that nice little barman I once met in Hong Kong to make you a few Bloody Marys to wash it all down.

We all need comfort foods. My own particular favourite is a chocolate fudge cake recipe that I've adapted from Tish Boyle; the main difference is that I've added an extra 24kg of chocolate and butter. Yummy. Serves one.

There will always be at least one day of the week when you don't fancy cooking and just want to slob out in front of the TV. And I'm willing to bet that it's the night that I'm on, so here's a few ideas that should mean you don't miss a second. How about chicken with chorizo and cannellini or Thai yellow pumpkin and seafood curry? Should only take 45 minutes or so.

Look, I can do trashy too. Just check out the cheeky Playboy rabbit I'm wearing. But all food to me is essentially a legacy of my childhood. I know for you this will invoke fishfingers and beans, but I'd like to leave you with some Italian sausages and lentils and liptauer to give you a taste of what a proper, decent home is like.

And that's all for now. I'm off to Chez Nico for *Vogue*. See you there.

The digested read ... digested

A third helping from the domestic goddess that should bring a warm, feelgood glow to everyone with kitchen staff.

Bushcraft

Ray Mears

No wilderness on this planet is more than four days' travel from your doorstep, but with your fat-cat expense accounts and your poncy villas in Tuscany, what would you care? Those of you who do venture outdoors once in a while would probably have a heart attack if your satellite phone went wrong. You've lost touch with the deeper knowledge of nature, but be mindful that – when your house is repossessed and your pension won't even buy you an almond croissant – if you can find shelter in the forest and know how to roast a hedgehog you will never be short of a home, hearth and meal.

First off you'll need some kit. A 100-litre rucksack is the bare minimum for anywhere outside the M25, as you'll need to carry clothes, navigational equipment, utensils, medicine and a large video recorder for making the documentary. Don't worry about food or something to sleep under as these can be taken care of on the way by staking out some marshes.

Wait till you see 500 geese feeding, then creep up on them and wring their necks. Start a fire by rubbing a piece of elder to create embers and then roast the goose at the equivalent of gas mark 6 for two hours. While this is cooking, pluck the remaining birds and stuff their feathers inside your trousers and shirt, having first tied off the legs and sleeves with lengths of cordage made from seaweed. You have now turned yourself into a duvet with a tog of 10.5.

Before settling down for the night, check you are not planning to go to sleep on the edge of a precipice, in a lion's den, down a crevasse or on the hard shoulder. Keep your fire lit to ward off mosquitoes and other dangerous predators.

If you know what you're doing you can easily construct a birch bark canoe in about half an hour, but as you don't you're going to have to think of other ways of crossing rivers. Your best option is to find a bridge; failing that look for where the water is shallowest. Prepare yourself for the cold water by taking a few cold showers before you leave home. If you have to swim across a deep expanse of cold water, a well-packed rucksack can be made into a pedalo.

Food deprivation is no laughing matter as you soon get hungry and grumpy. If you run out of goose, try looking for lobsters. If all else fails, there's fungi, burdock and lichen. And there you have it. You're ready for anything. So get lost.

The digested read ... digested

Everything you're unlikely to need for a tough night out on Clapham Common.

Minus Nine to One

Jools Oliver

I have to admit that it's always been my ambition to write a book and now my HUSBAND is a celebrity I can! I hope you find it as interesting as I do!

I have always wanted children since before I can remember, so I started talking to Jamie about having a BABY long before we met. Trying for babies is BRILLIANT fun of course, but we were both really disappointed when I did not get pregnant on our honeymoon. On one occasion I did think I might be pregnant as I developed a CRAVING for strawberry cheesecake. Unfortunately, it just turned out that I wanted to eat some strawberry cheesecake!

Because I had polycystic ovaries I was concerned I would be unable to conceive, so when I still wasn't PREGNANT after a month Jamie and I went to see one of the world's leading fertility experts. He gave me some drugs and told me to have sex. Because Jamie is so famous I had to arrange times with his PA to have SEX. I was going to say SHAG but my mum might read this! I love my MUM lots and lots. I love my dad, too. And my fabulous SISTER.

One day I woke up and found that my preganancy test was POSITIVE. I was so excited, I rushed out and spent loads of money on maternity clothes, but they didn't fit me till much later. Not many women realise you don't get FAT the moment you get pregnant. Before long I began to suffer from terrible morning sickness. This is when you are sick in the morning. It took me some time to work out what was going on because Jamie's FOOD used to make me feel sick anyway.

At first I only told my parents, my 100 best friends and *Hello!* that I was pregnant and I was deeply HURT that the tabloid newspapers found out about it and told the REST of the world before I could. But that's the price of being married to Jamie!

Before you have a baby, it's good to have a birth plan. Here's MINE:

1) Go to hospital.

2) Have baby.

It was great to come home with our darling Poppy, though it took a while to get used to the fact she was going to be in the house 24 hours a day. Thank goodness for my fantastic friends at the NCT. They were fantastic.

I struggled a bit with breast feeding to start with – cracked NIPPLES, yuk, don't go there! – and I was never very good at changing nappies. I hadn't realised babies needed to POO as well as eat. Luckily, Jamie is the best DAD in the world.

Within two months I was pregnant with Daisy, but I'm not going to write much about her as she's not that interesting. One of the best days was Poppy's first birthday, which just happened to fall on the same day she was born! WHAT a coincidence.

And that's it really. So lie back, run yourself a bath. And put the book in it!

The digested read ... digested

Pure saccharine from the Naked Mum.

The Privilege of Youth

Dave Pelzer

My heart was racing. I hadn't slept in days. I didn't even know what city I was in. I had never felt so lonely. But then it's tough when you're on a two-month lecture tour. The phone rang in my hotel room.

"Is that the world's most abused man?" asked the voice.

My blood ran cold and I answered in the affirmative. "I'm sorry to tell you that Dan Brazell has died."

Who was Dan Brazell? He was the man who had once fixed my bike, but I had yet to mention in print. Those three years I had never written about because they seemed too boring, suddenly assumed an unbearable poignancy. I could feel another book welling up inside me.

Everyone picked on me in school because I was in foster care. They could sense the abuse I had suffered and bullied me for it. But within days of my foster parents, the Welshes, moving to Duinsmoore Way, it felt as if a cloud was lifting from my tormented inner self. Here I met Dave Howard and Paul Brazell, the first two boys of my own age not to judge me for my lack of self-esteem.

After a few weeks I decided I could confide in them.

"You have to know," I whispered, "that I am the world's most abused person. My mother called me 'It', locked me in the cellar for days on end, set me on fire, made me eat ammonia, bombarded me with sub-atomic particles, ran me over with a steamroller and fed me to a great white shark."

"Actually, we'd read it all before in your other books," they yawned, "and we're bored stiff with hearing about it."

This was the acceptance I had always craved.

Paul, Dave and I did a lot of crazy things in those years. Occasionally we would break the speed limit and once I narrowly missed hitting someone when I lost control. "Wow," said Paul, "that was close." "Cool," said Dave. I had done something right in someone else's eyes.

I could feel my confidence rising and I once plucked up the courage to ask a girl out on a date. To my surprise I could sense she found me not unattractive and I bent forward to kiss her. Her mother rushed out and ordered me to leave. "Is it because I is abused?" I asked. "No," she replied. "It's because you're so boring."

Dave and Paul stayed on at school, but I felt the need to get a job. As a victim of abuse I still needed to prove myself. One day Paul moaned about his dad. I snapped. "Your dad is great he once fixed my bike. My dad never told me the three words I longed to hear: 'You are famous.'"

The three of us went our separate ways. I became a war hero before going on to critical acclaim as a professional victim. They amounted to nothing much.

At Dan's funeral, Paul asked me whether closure could ever be achieved. I checked my bank statement. "Not for the time being."

The digested read ... digested

The world's most abused man sinks to new lows of literary degradation.

Gordon Ramsay Makes it Easy

Gordon Ramsay

My name is Gordon Ramsay and I'm here to help. Simplicity has always been at the heart of my cooking and I'm going to show you how you too can become a star in the kitchen by learning how to boil an egg properly ... Oi, sonny, who the fuck are you? Get out of here. Who? You're my son? Fuck. I didn't recognise you.

Look, Gordon, we've got your kids in for the shoot to give you a cosier image, so do try to make it look like you spend time with your family.

There's nothing quite like a proper breakfast to start the day. I'm never at home myself, but I encourage the family to vary their breakfasts and make the most of seasonal fruit. So here's some easy-to-make recipes involving scallops, new potatoes and fresh cherry compote.

Fantastic, Gordon. OK, let's move on to the next chapter. Gordon, do you have to wear that pin-striped jacket? It really doesn't ....

Do you want to make something of it, you fuckwit?

No, No. You look absolutely splendid as you are.

Eating together as a family is important to me ... Fuck this. We're doing this fucking bollocks about how I love to eat Sunday roast with the family and they've all bleeding well fucked off.

It's OK, Gordon. I've given them a break, but we can get some lovely photos of you looking moody with some fish at the market.

Jesus. Right. Here's some fucking fillet of red mullet and here's some fucking roasted pork belly. Satisfied?

Er, perhaps you could try it with just a little more charm ...

When I'm relaxing at home in the summer, I invariably fire up the barbecue. Who writes this shit? Do you really think I've got the fucking time to sit around at home and fire up a fucking barbie when I've got restaurants to run, Michelin stars to protect and telly projects on the go?

I know, Gordon, but we're selling a lifestyle here. The punters need to think you're basically just like them.

Are you fucking mad? Do you really think I've worked my fucking guts out so I can have a fucking Corsa?

Please, Gordon.

OK. Let's just get this thing done. Right. Here's some seared tiger prawns and here's a lemon tart. Let's move on to party food. When Tana and I throw a party we never quite know how many we are catering for – not something you lot have to deal with, I know, but fucking get over it – so finger food and champagne cocktails are an easy option. What else? You want something posh? I'll fucking give you posh. The secret of a good halibut bourguignon is mastering the *cuisson*. Romance as well? We should all make time in our lives for romance. But I don't. Will that do?

Wonderful Gordon. Lights to fade and closing credits.

Alright lads let's hear it. Delia's going down, she's going down, Delia's going ...

The digested read ... digested

Gordo sells his sole.

Food Heroes: Another Helping

Rick Stein

It's hard to write about food heroes without mentioning myself first, but I will try to include a few other people along the way. My previous book, *Guide to the Food Heroes of Britain* (available from all good bookshops), listed producers of excellence, so this shameless attempt to cash in on my new TV series (on the BBC) will just list a few recipes from around the world.

Whenever I ask myself about the last time I enjoyed a meal that I hadn't cooked myself, I just draw a blank. Except for a pub in Devon that I like to patronise – in both senses of the word. As I've already said, I've written one cookery book and a guidebook and made a couple of TV series about it, but it never hurts to remind people. Especially when you're struggling to fill the space.

Those pictures of egg, cheese and pasta and pizza look yummy. I could have cooked them myself. Here's a recipe for an unusual dish – tomato, basil and mozzarella salad. And here's one from that great California chef, Alice Waters. I was going to visit her in September 2001, but the attacks on the World Trade Center and the Pentagon meant I had to cancel. It just goes to show that terrorism creates many more victims than you first imagine.

People ask me if I get tired of writing recipes. Of course I don't when there's so much easy money to be made. Want to make an ordinary salad look poncey? Just chuck in a few dandelions and cobnuts.

The most lyrical fishing I have ever experienced took place during the filming of *Food Heroes*. But I dare say that's not very interesting to you. I realised I hadn't done a recipe for *moules marinières* for ages – not since my first book, *English Seafood Cookery*, published by Penguin in 1986. So here's another.

I have been very keen in this book to make sure that all the ingredients for recipes are easy to get hold of because, unlike the first volume of *Food Heroes*, it doesn't include a list of specialist suppliers (instead they have been covered in the companion volume to this book, *Guide to the Food Heroes of Britain*). Is that clear enough?

Manel Trepte, Jeremy Stroud, Paul Flynn and Debbie, who helps me out from time to time. These chefs will mean nothing to you, so I don't mind giving them a mention. But back to me. Here's a recipe for the first dinner party dish I ever served, *la daube de boeuf provençale*, when I was just 21. It was a triumph then and it's a triumph now.

Though my name appears on the cover, this book is a team effort and I am indebted to many people. Unfortunately I've run out of room to list them other than in very small print that no one will be bothered to read.

The digested read ... digested

Me, me, me, me, me, me. The Rick Stein bandwagon keeps on rolling into a bookshop near you.

What Not to Wear

Trinny Woodall and Susannah Constantine

Don't we look gorgeous sitting together on the sofa? Don't we just ooze oomph? And we're here to tell you that you too can look nearly as fabulous as us. You won't be so rich or so posh, of course, and you'll probably call the sofa a settee, but if you follow our instructions you won't have to look quite so hideously common as you do now.

Don't feel too bad about yourself; even so-called celebs can get it wrong. Poor old Ulrika turned up at an awards ceremony and she was wearing her top back to front. Imagine that. She'd probably lost the flat-pack instructions from Ikea. Ha ha.

Sorry, we're being terribly rude. We haven't even introduced ourselves. I'm Trinny – or the tall thin one to you.

I'm Susannah, the short dumpy one.

Right let's get on with it. We may look divine, but we haven't always. Our secret is that looking good is all about avoiding the clothes you look crap in, rather than spending a fortune at Versace. Although obviously we're rich enough to do both.

Let me tell you that Trinny used to look a sight in Buck's-Fizz-meets-Spandau-Ballet evening wear, and you – and she – may think she has a fabuloso bod, but she's actually got short legs, no tits and a disproportionately large arse.

Thanks, Susannah, how about I tell the readers that underneath your oh-so-sexy, curvy figure is a stomach that needs stapling, hanging underarms and tits that are way too big for human handling?

There, now we've got that off our chest – and in Susannah's case that takes some doing – we can move forward. Because we must all be ruthlessly honest about our bodies before we can start to look good. So cut the crap of the fashion mags and learn like us to say words like arse, tits and bum. You're feeling better already, aren't you?

So here's a lot of piccies of clothes we think we look wonderful in next to a lot of piccies of clothes we look shit in. And you'll be able to tell the difference because we're smiling in the good clothes and looking grumpy in the rubbish ones. What a great idea that was. Must remember to thank our agent.

Er ... and that's all there is to it. Um, I know it's rather short, but could we stop now? We've got a couple of parties to go to. Ta-ra.

The digested read ... digested

What not to read.

Americana

Oracle Night

Paul Auster

Several months have passed since my near-fatal collapse, and my strength is slowly returning. My name is – it doesn't matter what my name is, but for the sake of correctness it is Sidney Orr.[1]

I go for my afternoon walk. The Brooklyn streets feel strange, yet strangely familiar. I come across a hitherto unknown shop, The Paper Palace. "You want some stationery?" asks the proprietor, Mr Chang. "This blue Portuguese notebook is just perfect," I tell him.

I am reminded of a conversation with my good friend, John Trause. "There is a story in Hammett's Flitcraft episode," he said. It has been a long time since I wrote anything, but I open the notebook and my pen glides across the page. There is this publisher, Nick. How much of him is me? He is married to Eva. How much of her is Grace?[2] Sylvia Maxwell's niece, Rosa, brings him the undiscovered manuscript of *Oracle Night*. He falls in love, and on the spur of the moment flies to Kansas. He meets a cab driver, Ed Victory. Is that his real name? No, it is Johnson, the name Grace calls my penis.

Grace says she looks in on my study while I am writing, but I am not there. I do not recall having moved. She reminds me it is time for dinner with John. "My phlebitis is very bad," he complains. I tell him about my notebook. "I was in Portugal once, and my favourite colour is blue," he says. "Be very careful."

I write through the night. Eva has cancelled Nick's credit cards. Rosa has picked up Nick's message on her answer machine.

Ed has died, leaving Nick trapped underground. I had written myself into a corner. I couldn't escape.

I go in search of another blue notebook, but The Paper Palace has closed down. I wander the streets and find another shop called the Paper Palace. There is Mr Chang. "You are my friend, Mr Sidney," he says. He takes me to a brothel. I find the black Haitian girl irresistible as she takes my penis in her mouth.

Grace is pregnant. "I must have an abortion," she cries. "But I want the baby," I reply. She sobs, before rushing out. "Trust me," she begs.

I go to see John. "You must be careful," he says. "Please visit my son Jacob in rehab." I go home and start writing. John and Grace had an affair before she met me, which was rekindled while I was in hospital. Is this how it was?

I hesitate to write the rest. Can the imagination make events happen? Mr Chang refused to sell me another notebook. Jacob came begging for money. We refused. He attacked Grace and she lost the baby. John sent me $36,000 shortly before he died of a pulmonary embolism. Jacob was found dead in Central Park. I saw myself tearing up the pages of the blue notebook.

1. Some people know me as Sid.

2. A reference to Grace Kelly? John called her Gracie, but not in homage to Gracie Fields.

The digested read ... digested

Old dog, old tricks.

Cosmopolis

Don DeLillo

He paced through his 48-room apartment, past the Borzoi cage, past the shark tank. The yen had risen overnight. Eric Packer didn't know what he wanted. Then he knew. He wanted a haircut.

"There's gridlock because the president's in town," said Torval, as the stretch limo pulled into the traffic."

"How do you know we're in the car and not in the office?" Eric snarled, staring at his bank of screens.

He glanced out the window. Was that his wife, Elise, the heiress? "I didn't know you had blue eyes," she said.

"When are we going to make love?" he replied.

Michael Chin got in the car. "I know where there's a Rothko for sale."

"I'll buy the whole gallery."

The car stopped to pick up his finance director, Jane Melman. "Your position on the yen is critical," she said.

"It can't go any higher," he answered, passing her a bottle to masturbate herself.

They stopped by Dr Ingram's surgery for his daily check-up. "Your prostate is asymmetrical."

Back en route, they passed a bookstore. Eric spied his wife again. "You smell of sex," she whispered.

"Have lunch with me."

"Is this what I wanted," she said, looking at her plate.

"I need a haircut."

Eric got back in the limo. The yen had to chart. He was the most powerful man in New York. He made the markets. He was like the famous novelist who could write utter crap and know that neither his editor nor the critics would notice.

They stopped by the apartment of Kendra Hays, his bodyguard. She kept on her Zyloflex body armour while they had sex. "Shoot me with your stun gun," he said. "I want to know how it feels."

He showed no curiosity when he bumped into Elise again. "My portfolio is valueless and someone is mounting a credible threat on my life."

"You still smell of sex."

He hacked into her account and stole $735m. Losing it was the best way of resisting it. "Why am I not interested in who wants to kill me?"

"Because no one else is," yawned Torval.

Anti-globalisation protesters sprayed paint on the car and a man set himself on fire.

"That's just not original," Eric said, while urinating.

The barbershop was closed, but Anthony came to him.

"Your hair is ratty."

"I knew it was time."

Elise walked through the door. "I've lost all your money," he said, as he straddled her.

"What do poets know of money? Our marriage is over."

Eric heard gunshots. He fired back.

"My name is Richard Sheets," said his assailant. "I hate you because you made me hate the baht."

Eric shot himself in the hand. "I've got an asymmetric prostate."

"So have I. But I've still got to shoot you."

The digested read ... digested

A Manhattan journey that is as deadly for us as it is for Eric.

A Heartbreaking Work of Staggering Genius

Dave Eggers

"You have to go into hospital, Mom." God. How long before she bleeds to death? "I'm not going." She's terrified she'll never leave as her cancer is end stage. She does leave, though, to go to Dad's funeral. A run-through for her own. A month later we're all back in church for hers. What do you do when both your parents die within 32 days, and you've just become the guardian of your 8-year-old brother, Toph? Play frisbee? Write a book? A cliche, I know, but at least it's not a screenplay. And check out that title. Postmodern or what?

The Chicago 'burbs hold nothing for us, so me and Toph head west to Berkeley. We're free to do whatever. Hang out on the beach, watch TV all hours, fart. No one can stop us. Toph is my laboratory. I can fill his head with my music, my books. He is one lucky, lucky guy. But he's my problem, too. I mean, looking after your 8-year-old brother is all very soulful, but how do you find the time to shag? When I'm not with him I worry someone's hacking him to death and when I am I just wish he'd fucking disappear and let me live my life.

You may not be interested in this next bit, as it's about Brent, Moodie, Jessica and the gang and our grungy low-life existence and our efforts to get *Might*, our avant-garde literary magazine, into the mainstream. I wouldn't blame you if you weren't, so just skip a few chapters.

I apply to be on the MTV show, *The Real World*. The interview is awesome; it goes like this – yeah, you've guessed. It doesn't, but it seemed a neat way of fitting in the autobiographical details that don't slot in elsewhere.

Contrived, but still neat, huh?

Oh, fuck, I'm dying. Who's going to look after Toph? False alarm. Kidney stone. But I do worry about dying a lot. Some of my friends actually do it. Where are my parents? I don't mean this philosophically, I mean it literally. They gave their bodies to research and I've lost track of them.

Hey, my mother's ashes have turned up and I scatter them on Lake Michigan. I go back to California, pull the plug on *Might*, and me and Toph move east to New York. Free. Finally.

The digested read ... digested

A moderately affecting work of basic competence.

Lake Wobegon Summer 1956

Garrison Keillor

Daddy is lying on the wicker daybed pretending to read *The Commentary to the Ephesians*; in reality he's listening to the Minneapolis Millers on the radio. I've just finished tending the lawn, with Fox's *Book of Martyrs* open on my knees. Tucked inside is a copy of *High School Orgies* lent to me by my friend Leonard.

"... revealed her orbs. Let me play with those puppies. My hand moved lower, where the heat blazed like a furnace."

"Just look at the boy," said Grandpa-up-in-heaven to Jesus.

"I can't do everything," grumbled Jesus.

I love this magazine – almost as much as I love my cousin, Kate. She's 16, two years older than me. Some times she doesn't wear a brassiere. I've written her a poem: *Kate, Kate / She's so great / I could wait eight hours straight / To attend a fête / For Kate.*

Kate's the only girl I've ever kissed. We were playing movie stars and her tongue slipped into my mouth.

Typically we were interrupted by my unpleasant sister. "I know what you've been reading," she says, "and I'm going to tell Mother and Daddy."

Denial. It's the only way. My parents are members of the Sanctified Brethren. I'm going to hell. Just look at this: "His manhood throbbed ...."

I'm a bright kid. At least everyone says I am. Other kids think I'm funny when I write poems about farting; still, it keeps me out of harm's way. I just yearn for Kate.

Kate's dating Roger, the starting pitcher for the Whippets. The local sports hack is on vacation and I've been asked to step in.

"… an auspicious sortie behooving incipient contenders as the Whippets thwarted the pliant Bards."

"I like your writing," said Roger. "Come out with me and Kate."

Her brassiere landed on the back seat beside me and a look of glazed satisfaction passed over Roger's face as her hand moved to his trousers. Had they forgotten I was there?

"I want *High School Orgies* back," said Leonard.

"I don't know what you're talking about," I replied. "I'm a writer now."

"Kate's pregnant," said Mother sadly.

As the wedding party ended, I went out alone to the baseball diamond and removed all my clothes.

"I worry about that boy," said Jesus.

The digested read … digested

Teenage whimsy
Feels quite flimsy.

The Plot Against America

Philip Roth

No childhood is without its terrors, yet I wonder if I would
have been a less frightened boy if Lindbergh hadn't been president
and I hadn't been a Jew.

We were a happy family in June 1940. My father was an
insurance salesman, my mother organised the PTA, my brother,
Sandy, was in high school and I was a 7-year-old stamp collector.
And then the Republicans nominated Lindbergh.

My father warned everyone he was a Nazi appeaser who would
persecute Jews. Rabbi Bengelsdorf said Lindbergh only wanted
peace for America and that we were Americans first and Jews
second. I had guilty dreams in which my Lindbergh stamps were
covered in swastikas.

Cousin Alvin had sharp suits and a too-sharp mind. He had
lived with us since his father died and he and my father had never
seen eye to eye over the company he kept. But they agreed over
Lindbergh. "I'm joining the Canadian army," he said. "I'm going
to fight in Europe."

Under the auspices of Just Folks – described by the Office
for American Absorption as a "volunteer program for city
youth to reconnect with the American heartland" – Sandy was
sent to live in Kentucky for a month. He came back having
eaten bacon and extolling the virtues of the Christian South.
My father was horrified. I was fascinated. Aunt Evelyn was
delighted. She had married Rabbi Bengelsdorf and was thrilled
to have been invited to the White House to meet General von
Ribbentrop.

Alvin came home with one leg missing in 1941. He slept in my room and I was fascinated by his stump. He gave me $20, which I kept hidden from my parents. It was my money for a rainy day. I was going to run away, but a horse kicked me in the head when I was little more than half a mile away. I would have died if Seldon hadn't found me. I didn't like Seldon, yet his saving my life tied us together.

"It's started," my father said, grimly. "My firm is sending me and the other Jews to different parts of the country. The persecution is coming." But he was a man of principle, and resigned. "I'd rather die in Newark." So in the event only Seldon and his mother went to Kentucky.

And then, over the course of the last 50 pages, everything got better. FDR decided to challenge for the presidency in 1944 and Lindbergh's plane disappeared. The vice-president was ousted after an illegal seizure of power, the Democrats took over the White House and Germany declared war on America. There were many theories about Lindbergh's disappearance. The British had taken him. The Nazis had taken him. No one knew.

There were riots against the Jews before FDR became president. My father drove to Kentucky to rescue Seldon after his mother was killed. At 42, that was his last action of the war.

The digested read ... digested

America then and now.

The Lovely Bones

Alice Sebold

My name is Susie Salmon. I was 14 when I was murdered on December 6, 1973.

My murderer was a man from our neighbourhood. My mother liked his flowers, but on a winter's afternoon Mr Harvey took me into a cornfield, raped me and then killed me.

When I first entered heaven I thought everyone could see what I see, but then I realised heaven was a place where everyone's wishes came true. Mine were of writing a bestseller.

Mr Harvey dumped my body down a sinkhole and all that the police found of me was my elbow. As my spirit floated up to heaven, I brushed past Ruth. She used to tell people she had felt my passing but no one ever believed her.

The main suspect for my killing was Ray Singh. He was exotic for our small town and I had been going to kiss him at school before Ruth interrupted us. But he had an unimpeachable alibi and Len Fenerman, the police detective, had to concede his innocence.

My father knew all along it was Mr Harvey. My sister Lindsey sensed it, too. Len Fenerman searched Mr Harvey's house but found nothing. "There's no evidence," he would explain patiently. My mother used to look at Len longingly.

Up in heaven I got to meet some of Mr Harvey's other victims. I also bumped into my grandfather. "How come I haven't met you before?" I asked.

"You will see more of me when you are ready to let go of Earth," he replied.

On the anniversary of my death, people from all over town gathered near where I died. It was their way of forgetting me. But my father couldn't. His obsession with Mr Harvey drove my mother into Len's arms. The only way she could cope was to leave home.

I watched Lindsey grow up and saw Mr Harvey leave town. One day my father had a heart attack and my mum came back from California. Ah! I also dropped into Ruth's body and let her float with the spirits of the dead while I finally got my kiss with Ray.

Mr Harvey died while trying to kill another girl and, in a peculiar symmetry that only happens in novels, his body remained hidden in the snow all winter.

I now only rarely visit Earth. I'm ready to explore what I call wide, wide heaven.

The digested read ... digested

Not even heaven remains untouched by the American way of schmaltz.

The Little Friend

Donna Tartt

For the rest of her life, Charlotte Cleve would blame herself for her son's death because she had decided to have the Mother's Day dinner at six in the evening instead of noon, after church, which is when the Cleves usually had it.

"Do I have to be in a book with such a clumsy opening sentence?" asked Harriett, Charlotte's petite, precocious 10-year-old daughter with the brown bob who bore absolutely no resemblance to the author.

"I'm afraid you do," replied her mother. "It's meant to convey the stultifying claustrophobia of a deeply dysfunctional family from Mississippi. Ever since your brother Robin was found hanged 10 years ago, your elder sister Allison and I have been in a catatonic state, and we're surrounded by a variety of misfits and inbreds."

"Hmm," said Harriett. "I'd better try to solve Robin's murder."

"Good idea," her friend Hely added. "I bet it was a Ratcliff. They're a bad lot and some of them have been in prison."

"You're right. I bet it was Danny. He was about the same age as Robin."

"There's a cage of poisonous snakes at Eugene Ratcliff's. Let's steal a cobra."

Harriett and Hely stood on the bridge. As Danny's car passed beneath, they tipped the cobra over the parapet.

"We almost killed Danny's granny," cried Harriett.

"Never mind," said Hely. "We didn't know she was driving the car."

"I shure doan trust those kids," yelled Farish Ratcliff, "an I shure doan trust you. Show me you've still got the drugs, or I'll kill you."

The drugs have turned him crazy, thought Danny, as he shot Farish in the head. Danny drove out to the water tower. Just get them drugs and get away, he told himself. Gosh, I miss Robin. I sure do wonder who killed him.

Harriett pulled open some of the packages. She didn't know what was in them but she knew Danny wouldn't like it.

"You brat, I'm going to kill you," Danny shouted, moments before he drowned.

"Get rid of all the evidence," Harriet begged Hely from her hospital bed.

"Poor old Harriett. Fancy having epilepsy," murmured her mother.

"You know Harriett had Farish shot and drowned Danny for killing Robin," Hely told his brother.

"You've been drinking too much coke."

The digested read ... digested

Small girl with big ambitions gets hopelessly confused in a laboured adventure. Still, she was very well paid for it.

Villages

John Updike

Julia eyes the sleeping Owen and marvels that after 25 years of marriage she is still so happy with him. Owen grunts and his hand reaches for his penis as he remembers the other women with whom he has shared his life. He is now 70 and his life can be measured out in the gentle golf swings of the semi-geriatric village of Haskell's Crossing.

His first village was Willow, Pennsylvania. What he really remembered was glimpsing the wispy curls of Doris's pubic hair. He made out with several girls in high school, but he didn't get his first real fuck until his second year at MIT. He met Phyllis on the computer coding course: she was in the year above and appeared impossibly out of reach until one day she said, "It's time we got engaged."

Owen got a job in New York working for IBM and soon had four children. A colleague named Ed suggested they go into business together, which is how he and Phyllis came to be living in the village of Middle Falls. Here the suburban curtains twitched day and night in rhythm with his sex life.

Faye was the first. She invited him for a drive in her car and they soon settled down into a quiet routine of adulterous monotony. Owen was neither happy nor unhappy, though his penis appreciated the exercise. He was never certain whether Faye had an orgasm or not, and in truth, such was the nature of his solipsism that he didn't much care. The affair fizzled out when Faye told her husband, who in turn informed Phyllis. But life in Middle Falls soon returned to normal as Phyllis understood she was past her prime and that a man had needs.

Within months there was Elsie. She demanded sex and Owen was happy to oblige. It was the 60s, the decade of free love, and Owen wasn't planning on paying. Phyllis continued to turn a blind eye to Owen, and Elsie turned a blind eye to contraception. Which was a mistake. Owen wondered briefly whether the baby might be his, but as with so much to do with his penis it was a case of onwards and upwards.

Ed's wife, Stacey, offered him a blow job and Owen was never sure why he declined. Maybe he was tired from his encounters with Alissa, Karen, Jacqueline, Antoinette and Mirabella. And Vanessa, who would do anything. She might even have agreed to a threesome, he remembered wistfully.

But it was Julia who changed everything. Perhaps Owen should have realised that fucking the pastor's wife would be a step too far for both Phyllis and Middle Falls. They told each other how much they loved one another even as the divorce was going through, but then Phyllis died in a car accident and Owen felt guilty.

He and Julia moved to Haskell's Crossing, and for the last 25 years he has only played with her. And himself.

The digested read ...digested

Rabbit keeps on vibrating.

I am Charlotte Simmons

Tom Wolfe

"Well, ah-ull be darned," said Charlotte's mother, "Fancy a hillbilly's daughter go-un to Dupont."

Charlotte grimaced at the way her mammy said ah-ull and go-un. She wished she would shut up. "I am Charlotte Simmons," she said to herself.

The cleverest girl ever to leave Sparta, North Carolina felt crippled inside. Her roommate was so posh.

"So here we are in our fuck-pad," grinned Beverley. "Can I use all the cupboard space? You don't have any clothes."

Charlotte bit her tongue. "I am Charlotte Simmons," she said to herself. She had never been amongst people who cussed. She looked down at her floral dress. At least it covered her breasts, whatever they were. Charlotte knew men might want to touch them, but she didn't know why as she had never read Cosmopolitan. "I am Charlotte Simmons," she said to herself.

Jo-Jo Johanssen felt out of place. The previous year he had been on the starting line-up for the basketball team but now he had been replaced. "Snot fair," he whined. He rang Adam. "Come oder and do my history paper," he barked.

Adam Gellin hated the sports jocks and the frat boys: but most of all he hated himself. He was one of the brightest boys on the block, yet he had to cover for Jo-Jo.

"Bad news," whispered Jo-Jo, later. "Mr Quat finks somewun else dun my essay as it's got words he dudn't fink I kno."

If Adam was caught helping Jo-Jo his chances of a Rhodes scholarship were over. "H-h-help," he sobbed.

"I tell u wot ahma gonna do. I've met this girl Charlotte an she finks I'm not as stupid as I finks I am, so I'm gonna learn about Socrates."

Adam, too, had heard of Charlotte and loved her for her mind.

Over in the frat room, Hoyt Thorpe was feeling pleased with himself. Not only had he been offered a job as a bribe to keep his mouth shut over the blow job Syrie gave the governor of California but Charlotte was going with him to the frat formal. "She's gonna be my cum dumpster."

Rutrutrutrutrut. Charlotte could not believe Hoyt had abandoned her. The vodka had affected her and she had allowed herself to be penetrated. She was a laughing stock. "I am Charlotte Simmons," she said to herself.

Adam enjoyed taking Charlotte under his wing, but was distressed she only thought of him as a friend. Still, life was not too bad. Quat dropped the plagiarism charge after he exposed Hoyt. A Pulitzer prize beckoned.

Jo-Jo was once more king of the court and he even knew how to spell his own name. It was all down to Charlotte. She'd saved him.

Charlotte looked around the arena. People envied her, but she felt a little distant. It was time to start behaving like Jo-Jo's girlfriend.

The digested read ... digested

I'm not as good as I used to be.

Lad lit

The White Stuff

Simon Armitage

Felix sighed. It was so difficult watching lad lit try to grow up. The blokeish humour seemed so stale when there were so many important issues to deal with. Still, he was a social worker, so he was used to dealing with issues.

"I'm still not pregnant," huffed Abbie, his wife. "I don't think you begin to realise how important having a child is when you're adopted and you don't know who your real parents are."

The weekly casework meeting passed off uneventfully. The other social workers were all *Private Eye* stereotypes, but Felix felt smug that he, at least, had two dimensions. He looked at the latest case file. It was from Abbie, asking for help in tracking down her parents. "This is highly irregular," he said to her later, "but as this is not a very good book, I'll let it pass. I have to warn you, though, there could be big issues surrounding the search. You could have been born as a result of a rape."

"That would be a very big issue," Abbie conceded. "But I have to know anyway."

Felix spoke to the adoption agency. Phew. Abbie wasn't born as the result of a rape. Her mother was a Maria Rosales. He tried the phone book. No luck. He checked the death register. Bingo.

"I'm afraid we've reached a dead end," he said wittily. "Never mind, we're going to dinner with Maxine and Jed."

"Our two kids are such a handful, sometimes we'd do anything to get rid of them," laughed Maxine and Jed.

How unbearably ironic that is, thought Felix. Here's a couple who have children and don't want them, and here we are wanting children and not being able to have them. That must count as another issue.

"I'm ovulating," Abbie announced. Felix was finding it difficult to rise – Arf! Arf! – to the challenge.

"I can't do this any more," he confided to Jed. "Now she wants to do IVF, and I'm expected to provide a specimen. Please help me by doing it for me."

"You're kidding," Jed said. "That's the most ridiculous storyline I've ever heard."

"Wait till you see what's coming. In any case, Abbie won't get pregnant, so that strand will die quietly."

The distance between Felix and Abbie grew steadily wider. Having a baby was an even bigger issue than Felix imagined. "We don't talk any more," Abbie complained. "You didn't tell me you saved a girl during a fatal shooting."

"It seemed pointless. It was only a ropy sub-plot."

Felix watched the school reunion video. There was a girl with the same characteristics as Abbie. She must be related. They rushed round to visit a pregnant Mrs Hardison. "Oh yeah," she said. "You've got the same dad as my kids."

Two months later, Abbie came home with a baby. "Mrs Hardison's given me hers. So I'm now going to be mother to my father's child." Felix reached for the door, but the readers had beaten him to it.

The digested read ... digested

It's life, Felix, but not as we know it.

High Society

Ben Elton

"My name's Tommy Hanson and I'm an addict." The NA meeting went quiet. "I guess you all know that. Well since I won *Pop Hero*, I've had tonnes of drugs and loadsa birds. Did ya see me at the fuckin' Brits? So out me fuckin' head I even dumped that posh bird out me fuckin' limo on the way."

* * *

"Gosh, ya, Emily here. Well, once Tommy had thrown me out of the limo in the middle of Brixton, I got into a few scrapes I can tell you. But I won't bore you with the details, as I'm only here to show it's much easier for rich people to come off drugs than poor people."

* * *

Peter Paget straightened his tie as he entered the House. Today he was going to make a name for himself. "I propose that all drugs be legalised. The war on drugs has been lost, and it would better for all of us if we admitted it."

"Boo! Hiss! You're a disgrace," shouted everyone in the House.

* * *

"Ooh, you're the best, Peter," said Samantha, his assistant. "Have some coke and fuck me."

"Why doesn't my wife treat me like this?"

"Do you mind if I call you Daddy?"

* * *

Jessie lay back and took her fourth punter of the day. Life was tough when you were a 15-year-old smackhead from Scotland.

"I don't want tae be a whore," she thought. "I want tae be clean."

* * *

The PM picked up the phone. The whole country was getting behind Paget. It was time to put him in the cabinet.

* * *

"How dare you dump me, Daddy," yelled Samantha. "I'm going to go to the press and tell them about our affair."

"I'll deny it," Paget replied. "I'll say you were trying to derail the most important drugs reforms in history."

"Ya boo, you're a lying slapper, Paget is our hero," ran all the headlines.

* * *

"We've changed our minds," said everyone. "You're a cheat."

"It was a stupid idea to change the drugs laws," said the PM. "You're fired."

* * *

"Like I meet this top Scottish bird in a fuckin' brothel an' we get clean together an' I takes her away on holiday."

* * *

"My name's Ben Elton. Good night."

The digested read ... digested

Not even industrial quantities of drugs can raise a pulse in lifeless cardboard cut-outs.

A Long Way Down

Nick Hornby

Martin: Can I explain why I wanted to jump off a tower block? I'd been to prison for having sex with a 15-year-old girl – yeah, I know what you're going to say, but she told me she was older – I'm separated from my wife and kids, I lost the big TV job and all in all I'm a bit unhappy.

Maureen: I picked New Year's Eve because it seemed like a good idea. I told Matty I was going to a party, but he looked blank.

Jess: Like, I was at this party looking for Chas who had dumped me, like, and I remembered the block was called Topper's Tower, so I, like, thought, whateffer.

Martin: These two women appeared next to me and we sat and chatted for a bit about jumping and then this other bloke turned up.

JJ: I don't know why I decided to kill myself, really. Sure, my girlfriend had left me and my rock band had split up, but this was everyday stuff for a superannuated everybloke from north London. In the end, I guess it was just that I didn't think the book would work with only three voices as we'd never sell the film rights unless I pitched up, too.

Maureen: After so many years of looking after my disabled son by myself, it was quite nice to get together and chat about killing ourselves.

Jess: Like, I persuaded them dull fuckers to go to this party where I thought that bastard Chas would be.

Martin: I might have guessed that idiot Chas would recognise me and tell the papers that we had all met up on Topper's Tower.

Jess: Fuckin' fantastic. I persuaded some fick journo it was an angel wot had persuaded us not to jump and she's, like, given us all loadsa money for the story.

Maureen: It was quite nice to talk to a journalist. I still feel a bit guilty about Matty, though.

JJ: I haven't said anything for a while, so I thought I'd check in. I've been making lists of pop groups, you know. I find that very interesting.

Martin: Oh God, the story just gets worse. It turns out that Jess is dead posh and is the daughter of the education minister. I should have topped myself when I had the chance.

Jess: Like, I hate my parents. And they, like, hate me too. It's *soo* unfair. I suggested we all spend the dosh going to Tenerife, and I got well smashed for a week.

Maureen: I loved Tenerife. I'd never been abroad before.

JJ: Jess arranged for us all to meet up with the important people in our lives. I now go busking and am happier than I've ever been.

Martin: I realised my life was shallow and I now help disadvantaged kids to read. It's so cathartic, I'm never going to think about killing myself again.

Jess: I've got a new boyfriend and I adore my parents.

Maureen: I go to quiz nights and we're all going to remain really good friends.

The digested read ... digested

The only genuine despair is the reader's.

Man and Wife

Tony Parsons

I look at my wife, Cyd. Cyd, my wife. I look at. Wife my. Cyd at. Look. I.

I hate the fact I have to call her my second wife. Really. Hate. It. She is. My best. Wife. Not like that. Slug fat. Fat slug. Gina. First. Wife. My.

I. Don't. Know. Why I. Write in. These ridiculous. Sentences. And repeat. Re. Peat. Mys. Elf. Now. To women. Know I hate. The poncey. Middle-classes. That. Watch the. Late. Review.

I. Really. Love Pat. He's my son. Pat I. Love. He's the. Best. Thing. I've ever. Done. Best. The. It breaks. My heart. That he. Lives. With. Gina. And her. Equally slug-like. New squeeze. Richard. Heart. My. Bre. Aks.

Here's. My. Mum. She's the. Best. Mum. The. Of . Earth salt. "I've got cancer, Harry," she. Rasps. Just like. My dad. Who passed. On a couple. Of ago. Years. He was the. Best. Of earth. Salt.

"Richard and I are moving to the US," says. Gina. She can. Almost manage. Manage almost. A. Sentence.

I cry. I. Weep. Sob. I. "I'll hardly. See. Pat." Comforts. Cyd tries. But she. Love doesn't. Pat. Like. Do. I.

Gina shows. Me some photos. Of Pat that. A friend of. Hers. Called Kazumi. Took. Me. Astonishingly. Aston. Ishing. Ly. I Kazumi. Meet. After soon. "Let's have. Affair. An," I. Say. She kisses. Tenderly. Me. "But you can't sleep with me," adds. She.

Love. Cyd doesn't. Me. Any. More. I'm sure she's. Fucking. That bloke. Who wants. Business. Her to. Buy. Her daughter. Peggy. Peg. Gy. Her marriage. First from. Me. Hates.

"Pat and I are coming back to England," whimpers. Gina. "Richard and I are separating."

"I'm doing all right, son," gasps. Mum. My. The best. She's.

"I'm not having an affair," Cyd. Says. "But I want to leave before you do. You need to sort your life and grammar."

A knocks. Car. Down Peggy. I rush. The to. Hospital. Than rather. Kazumi. Called. It's cathar. Sis.

"Richard and I will try again," gushes. Gina. "Let's be better parents to Pat."

And I. Cyd. Are go making. Another. It of. She's. Best. The. The rings. Phone. Gina it's. "Kazumi has just got married."

All loose. Tied ends up. One. Except. "I'm pregnant," says. Cyd. I believe. Can't. My luck. That. Buy. People. This. Shite.

The digested read ... digested

A. To tackle. Book. Syntax your. But. Your not. Brain. Brai. N. Br. Ain. Bra. In.

Chick lit

Sorting Out Billy

Jo Brand

Martha had never progressed much beyond hating her father
for being cruel to her and her mum, even though he was supposed
to be a man of God. Martha was now 38 and eight months
pregnant. She told everyone that she didn't know who the baby's
father was, but she knew perfectly well it was Ugly Ted, who
owned the lapdancing club.

"I'm really feisty, me," she said, meaning the opposite. Inside,
she was just an insecure girl looking for love.

There was a knock on the door. "Hi," said Flower, a skinny
hippy who never said anything interesting or funny, yet managed
to be offered endless stand-up gigs. "Billy's beaten up Sarah."

"You've got to leave him," they both said to Sarah.

"I fell down the stairs," lied Sarah. She longed to tell the truth
but could not be disloyal to the man she loved.

"She's locked into a typical cycle of domestic violence," Martha
intoned sagely.

Flower confronted him. "You've got to stop being mean
to Sarah," she whispered, when really she wanted to shout
at him.

"Fuck off," replied Billy, who really wanted to say how sorry
he was and that he was the victim of abusive parents.

There then followed 100 pages of hilarious comedic set pieces.
Flower sent her boyfriend to investigate an anger management
class and he ended up getting beaten up! Martha and Flower went
to a self-defence class run by a wimp, accidentally killed someone
in the pub (still no harm done!) and then got threatened on the

bus only to be saved by the self-defence wimp, who beat up six teenagers! My, how we almost chuckled.

"My gags are falling as flat as the dialogue in this book," said Flower.

Well, at least they're better than the descriptive passages, thought Martha.

"Billy's beaten up Sarah, again," Flower continued. "I'm going to buy a gun."

"Let me sort him out," Martha offered.

Billy grabbed her and held her close. Within seconds they were fucking. "What have I done?" cringed Martha, whereupon she promptly fucked him again.

"This is just unbelievable," said Flower.

Twelve hours later, Martha was holding her son. "Wouldn't it be hysterical to call him Jesus to piss off my dad?" she laughed. Ugly Ted was initially a little upset to find out he was the dad, but soon got over it. "We're a family now," he and Martha said.

It was Flower's last chance at comedy. She had been given a pill to relax her, but it turned out to be an amphetamine! She pulled out the gun. "You've got to be nicer to Sarah," she shouted at Billy.

"I love her, really," Billy said, vulnerable for the first time. "I want to change."

"We all love each other," slurred Flower.

"Put the gun away", Martha yelled.

"No," the last remaining reader cried. "Use it on me."

The digested read ... digested

Stick to the day job.

Olivia Joules and the Overactive Imagination

Helen Fielding

"Perhaps you'd be better on the style section than on news," said the foreign editor of the *Sunday Times*. "Why don't you go to Miami to cover a beauty launch?"

It was just so not fair, Olivia thought. She so wasn't an airhead. (Memo to self: Three pages knocked off.)

Miami was sweltering in the heat as Olivia lay on the beach in her D&G bikini. "Allo, darlink," said a tall swarthy Arab pretending to be a Frenchman.

"Ohmygod!" Olivia shrieked down the phone to Kate. "I've met an Arab, he's bound to be in al-Qaida."

Down at the port a cruise ship blew up. "I knew Feramo was so a terrorist," Olivia thought to herself. "I'm going to follow him to LA." (Memo to self: 65 pages = one-fifth of an advance.)

"You keep your hands off Feramo," warned the tanned and languid Suraya.

"I wanna kees you, Olivia," smooched Feramo.

"Ohmygod Kate!" she shrieked down the phone. "He's definitely a terrorist."

"It all seems a bit feeble to me," Kate replied.

Olivia started crying. "It"s not my fault. I didn't write this shit." (Memo to self: No idea where story is going. Could try Honduras.)

"Comea weetha me to Honduras," whispered Feramo.

Honduras was very hot, Olivia thought, but the diving was nice. She snogged Morton, the diving instructor.

"Aaagh," she yelled at Morton. "First I see a floating head

underwater and now you're taking me to Feramo. I'm trapped in an international terrorist conspiracy."

Feramo flashed his tongue at her. God he was irresistible. "I so want to go home," she wept.

Back in London, Kate introduced her to one of the top MI6 controllers. "Meet two of my other operatives – Suraya and Scott, aka Morton." Olivia blushed. She had so snogged Morton. Being an Arab, Feramo was a terrorist, and MI5 needed Olivia's help to catch him.

Olivia fondled the cyanide pills in the lining of her Wonderbra. (Memo to self: Editor is desperate for manuscript. Any old tosh will do.)

"Feramo's just phoned to invite me to go diving in Sudan," Olivia said.

"We'll be keeping an eye on you," said Scott.

Feramo captured Olivia and took her to his base. "I've lost an earring," she said. She had to escape. She opened an electronic door. A helicopter flew overhead. "Thank you for saving me, Scott."

"Thank God we've saved the world from terrorism," Scott muttered.

"Not quite," Olivia replied. "They've put a bomb in the Oscars. Brad's in danger."

"You've saved the civilised world again." (Memo to self: Get out of country before reviews appear.)

The digested read ... digested

Helen Fielding and the Overpressing Deadline.

Shopaholic & Sister

Sophie Kinsella

I'm a bit of an expert at this meditating lark now. The guru wants me to walk on hot coals.

"Do you think I could wear my six-inch stilettos?" I ask Lukey-wukey.

My husband pulls at his blond plaits and says, "I think it's time we went home."

He's right. We've been everywhere on our 10-month honeymoon and I've bought lots of exciting things, but I can't wait to get back to my Manolos. "Do you think we could stop off in Milan for shopping on the way home?"

"Sounds great, Becks," says Lukey-wukey. "I need to go there to prepare for our pitch for the Arcodas PR account."

I'm feeling so guilty. I've just spent £2,000 on an Angel bag with a credit card Lukey-wukey knows nothing about. I had to. This nice man Nathan got me to the top of the waiting list!

It's horrible to be back in England. My best friend Suze has got a new best friend, Lulu; Lukey-wukey has cut his hair and works too hard and I don't have enough money to go shopping. Even Mummy-wummy and Daddy-waddy have been hiding something from me. Grrr!!!

"We've just discovered Daddy-waddy had another daughter from a previous girlfriend," said Mummy-wummy.

I've got a sister. "How fantastic is that," I say, because I'm too shallow to think through the consequences.

Jessica is so weird. She doesn't like shopping and saves money!! I still think we'll be best friends, though.

Oh gosh, Nathan's just rung up asking whether Lukey-wukey could do the PR for his new hotel in Cyprus. I can feel a party coming on. How fabby is that!!

"Nathan is a crook," says Lukey-wukey. "Not the sort of client we need now we have the Arcodas account. Why can't you be more like Jessica?"

Wah! It's not fair. Lukey-wukey prefers Jessica, and he even left to go on a business trip without giving me a snoggy. My marriage is over.

I am oop north outside Jessica's house. "Teach me to be more like you," I plead.

"I don't like you and we're probably not related anyway."

I can't stop crying in the local shop. Still, the assistant likes my make-up and Jessica's father takes me to see her rock collection. She keeps them in the same cupboard I keep my shoes in!! We must be sisters. I rush to tell her.

I've fallen down a cliff and lost my Angel bag, but me and Jessica are now nearly best friends. Well, we would be if Suze hadn't appeared to say she was still my best friend really, and Lukey-wukey's phoned to say he loves me and was wrong about Nathan.

Jess has persuaded me to turn environmental and I'm running the campaign to stop the new shopping development. Oh my God, it's Lukey-wukey. The development belongs to Arcodas. Help!!! Oh, Arcodas aren't going ahead anyway, so everything's great after all. And I'm pregnant!!!

The digested read ... digested

A treatise on the dangers of inbreeding among the terminally dim.

Don't You Want Me?

India Knight

"Nnyurgh. Aaah. Come on my face."

I don't want to be listening to this. It's two in the morning, I've got to be up at six when Honey wakes up, and Frankie's going hammer and tongs with his latest squeeze.

I expect you're wondering what a 38-year-old single mother is doing sharing a house with a sex-obsessed ginger lodger. No? Well, I'm going to tell you anyway as it's the easiest way for someone with minimal plotting skills to fill in the back story.

Here goes. I'm very bohemian, posh middle-class. I got married to Rupert when I was in my early twenties and we divorced soon after. I met Dominic when I was 34. We didn't get married, but we did have Honey. Dom buggered off with a Japanese woman.

And here I am. And Frankie? He's one of Dom's artists, but don't worry about this being one of those "the right man was under my nose all along" books, because he's got ginger pubes. Yuck. And he's got a child he never contacts.

"Do you think I'll ever have sex again?" I ask Frankie.

"You need to get out more," he says.

Time to take Honey to her playgroup. Oh, there's the revolting Ichabod, and the thoroughly wet Castor and Pollux. You're right, we're in PC north London. The old stereotypes are always the best, I think. Ah, there's Louisa. "Come back to my place and have a glass of chardonnay," she giggles. "You can meet my neighbour."

"Yo skankin," he says.

"That's Adrian," Louisa explains, "though he prefers to be called Youngsta. He's a DJ."

"Very pleased to meet you," he continues, slipping into perfect RP.

Take away the Ali G suit and Youngsta is drop-dead gorgeous. "Why don't we go on a double-date. You and Frankie, me and Adrian?" I say later.

Adrian is on the decks. "I don't do drugs," I announce, hoovering up some coke, before closing in on Frankie.

"Fuck me, Frankie," I beg.

"No."

"Go on."

"OK."

"What about your child?" I ask in post-coital bliss.

"I don't have a child. Dom must have made it up to put you off me, I love you."

Oh, so it is one of those books where the right man was under my nose all along. *Quelle surprise*.

The digested read ... digested

No, we don't.

Dot.homme

Jane Moore

He's tall, dark and handsome with a chiselled jaw. "Hi," I shout. He looks blank. It is him, I'm sure it is. "You look just like your photo," I say.

"Well you don't look anything like yours," he snaps.

How did I get into this situation? Let me explain.

It was my 34th birthday. My friends had gathered for a surprise party. Some surprise! "Look what I've got you," said Kara, whom I've always hated, though she did once save me from drowning. "I've placed an ad for you with an online dating agency. "Desperate thirtysomething nearing sell-by date. Any offer considered."

My heart sank. All my friends were either married or in relationships. There was my perfect sister, Livvy – her marriage was so perfect you could tell something bad was going to happen shortly. Then there were Tab and Will, and my two obligatory cliched camp gay friends.

And me. Single, working as a researcher for a morning TV makeover show. So I went on a few dates. Most were neanderthal Ross Kemp types I ran a mile from, and then there was the gorgeous Simon who dashed out of the restaurant, leaving me to pay.

"He must have been married," I say to Livvy.

"I've got some bad news," she replies. Were she and Michael splitting up? "I've got breast cancer."

"Gosh, that makes my problems seem rather small. I'm going to do something worthwhile with my life."

My phone rang. "I'm Ben, a friend of Will's. I run a hospice for children. I wonder if you could give a makeover to one of our tireless workers whose son recently died of leukaemia."

"OK. Let's meet for a drink."

Ben was good-looking in an understated, sensitive way. "It must be very hard for you to deal with your sister's illness issues," he lisps caringly.

"Don't get too involved," Will warns me. "I saw him hugging another man at the rugby club. Definitely gay."

My flame-haired boss calls me into her office. "No more of that wishy-washy stuff on my programme."

"Well, you can stuff your job," I flounce.

Back home, I find an email from Simon. "Sorry about last time. I was married but now I'm not. Let's meet again."

He looks as gorgeous as ever. "Bad news about your sis, old girl," he barks. "Now get those stockings off."

Yummy sex, but surely there should be more to a relationship than this.

Another email appeared from a man named Ben. "I'd like to get to know you properly before we meet." We chatted for weeks online, before he invited me to dinner.

It was Ben! "I'm not gay," he says. "I was caring for a man whose partner was dying."

I was the happiest girl alive.

It was my 35th birthday.

"I'm in remission and doing well," says Livvy.

"The IVF worked," says Tab. "I'm pregnant."

"Will you marry me?" squeaks Ben.

The digested read ... digested

Deidre's photo casebook. Without the photos.

I Don't Know How She Does It

Allison Pearson

1.37am: Why am I up at this time of night distressing the M&S mince pies for Emily's carol concert when I've got to fly to New York first thing? Because I can't trust Rich to do it. And why's he called Rich when he earns less than the nanny? Come to think of it, why am I called Kate Reddy, my boss Rod Task and my email flirtee Jack Abelhammer? Oh, I see, I've got into one of those books where people's names describe their characters in a terribly amusing way.

8.52am: Sorry about that, I've got a bit more time to chat now I'm in midair. So what do you need to know? I'm a fund manager with Ernest Morgan Foster; I've got two gorgeous kids, Emily and Ben, whom I feel tremendously guilty about. Ah, that reminds me. There, I've just ticked all the boxes for the Hamleys catalogue. Now where was I? Ah yes, all men are useless. Things to remember: cancel the stress-busting massage.

6.03am: Just back from New York. Almost had sex with Jack. Rich tries to bully me into a reunion shag, but I pretend to fall asleep. "We need to talk," he says later. "Don't you realise I've got a very important presentation in 50 minutes?" I reply. Life is so much tougher for women.

10.49am: Presentation interrupted by the arrival of my dad. The loser needs some money. "Will £10K do?" I snap. Why does every mega-woman have a useless father? Why can't I have an easy life earning the same mega-bucks churning out dreary columns or chatting to Tom and Tony?

2.42pm: Momo and I won the right to manage the ethical fund. Hooray. Rich has left home. The nanny's gone Awol. A colleague's wife has died, adding pathos and poignancy to my predicament.

7.10pm: My kids fail to recognise me.

7.12am: Momo discovered some porno pics of her were doing the rounds at work. Persuade hated male colleague who did this to invest in my dad's project, thereby paying off his debts and wasting EMF's money.

9.15am: Resign from EMF. Sell house, move to Derbyshire to return to honest working-class roots. Am back with Rich, kiss kiss. Never did shag Jack, boo hoo. The kids have never been happier. And who's this at the door? My sister Julie, saying the local doll's house factory is about to close. Do I spot an opportunity?

The digested read ... digested

A passingly amusing newspaper column mistakenly allowed to get totally out of hand.

Stupid Cupid

Arabella Weir

Hat was reeling. Like, literally reeling. She was so stunned she was sure she was going to fall over.

"I just cannae do it," Jimmy Mack had just said in his best it's-not-you-it's-me voice.

"But we've already sent out the invitations and booked the church and the caterers," she replied.

Jimmy Mack shrugged helplessly in his best I-would-do-something-about-it-if-I-could manner.

"So what are you going to do?" asked Mish a little later.

"I'm not going to tell a soul," said Hat. "There's still six weeks till the wedding, I'm sure he's just got an attack of last-minute nerves."

"That's the silliest idea I've ever heard," replied Mish in her best I'm-indulging-you-now-but-I won't-for-much-longer voice.

A week later Hat was back at Mish's flat. "Oh Mish, it's all going wrong," wailed Hat. "First off, my plan to boil his toy bunny went wrong and then I dressed up in my sexiest lingerie and tied myself to his bed only to find he's gone to Scotland and has a lodger staying. And to cap it all, my sister Penny with the perfect marriage and my parents have invited me and Jimmy to dinner."

"Well," said Mish in her best no-problem's-too-big-for-us voice, "we'll have to get Sam to stand in for Jimmy. Your family haven't met either of them."

"But isn't he married to that glamorous South American woman, Gloria?"

"Yes, but she won't mind, I'm sure," replied Mish enigmatically.

"Oh gosh, that was such a jape," laughed Sam as they drove home after dinner. Sam wasn't at all like Jimmy Mack, Hat thought. He was so sensitive, so emotionally available and his eyes were just to die for.

"Oh Hat," wailed Penny. "Don't go through with it. I might look like I have the perfect marriage but I don't really love Guy even though he is a lord's son."

Hat looked at the empty pews on the groom's side. This is madness, she thought.

Just then, Jimmy Mack ran into the church. "I do," he gasped.

"I do-n't" stuttered Hat. "I'm sorry Jimmy Mack. I don't love you."

"I love you Hat," whispered Sam. "You do realise that my marriage to Gloria is just one of convenience. She's a gay-rights activist and I helped her get out of the country."

His tongue darted into Hat's mouth. "I love you too," she whooped.

The digested read ... digested

Forget the Cupid, just think Stupid.

Beyond belief

The Face

Garry Bushell

"You fuckin' poncin' slag," shouted Pyro Joey, as he nutted the Kosovan illegal immigrant.

"Leave it out," laughed Rhino, pissing on the unconscious body. "We've got a meet with Johnny Too down the Ned."

The Ned Kelly in Rotherhithe was the flagship of Johnny and Joey Baker's empire, but everyone knew it was Johnny who was The Man.

"Listen up, bruv," said Johnny, as he carved out a few lines of charlie with his gold card. "We're going for the big one." And if all goes well, he thought, it'll be the last time I get my hands dirty. The others can do the graft from then on and I'll be untouchable. Except to that tart Geri; she can touch me any time.

"Right," barked DCI Hitchcock. "If we don't nail the Bakers soon, we never will. We want you to go in, Tyler."

"No probs, guv," replied Harry Tyler, the Met's top undercover cop.

A few days later Harry had settled into his new flop in Stratford, and was shagging Elaine, the next-door neighbour. It was good cover, he reckoned, and it gave him a bit of exercise.

"Fancy a beer?" Harry asked Pete, one of the faces in the Baker gang. "By the way, I've also got some moody Scotch at three sovs a bottle. Interested?"

"There's someone you should meet," whispered Pete.

"Who the fuck are you?" demanded Johnny, after Pete brought Harry along to the Ned. "I do a bit of this, bit of that. Duckin' and divin', yer know."

"Wot do you fink of *Guardian* readers?"

"All poofs and gobshite lefty cunts."

"And wot's yer best paper."

"You takin' the piss? The *Sun*, o'course."

"You're all right, my son. You're a good un. Have a drink."

"I'd rather have the barmaid."

"Help yerself."

"Wot are you havin'?" smirked Lesley, the barmaid.

"Your tits, for a start," Harry quipped.

"Fuck me, Johnny, me knob's really sore after that Les."

"Never mind vat," said Johnny. "You're coming wiv me to the Dam to arrange a shipment of 50Ks of charlie."

Ten days later, Scotland Yard's crack armed response team nicked the whole Baker gang as they unloaded the charlie at Rotherhithe docks.

"That cunt Harry's dead," yelled Johnny as he went down for 15 years. Johnny became a born-again Christian and a *Guardian* columnist.

The digested read ... digested

Witless, plotless gangster pulp fiction that manages to insult almost everyone, especially the readers.

The Man with the Dancing Eyes

Sophie Dahl

In the golden half-light of a midsummer's evening, the sort where any kind of magic can occur, lay Pierre, naked on a bed, except for her Christian Louboutin shoes. Nobody knew where she came from or what she did and assumed she must be fantastically interesting. But in fact she wasn't. She was just a model.

Pierre felt a tap on her shoulder and found herself staring into the dancing eyes of a 73-year-old pop star. "Ya dahn't wahnt ma traasers ta fahll dahwn naw, da ya," he said in his comical, faux working-class voice.

"Oh, it's you," she whispered, as she melted into his eyes.

"S'raht, babe."

Pierre and the geriatric with the dancing eyes waltzed off into the night, drinking oceans of champagne. They kissed as the sun came up over Albert Bridge, and the geriatric played her a song he had written long before she was born.

The geriatric with the dancing eyes and Pierre went to a multitude of parties during a long Saga weekend in Frinton. "I love you," Pierre cooed. "Let's settle down, buy an Aga and have babies."

But the geriatric grew restless.

"Angie, dahn't ya weep," he warbled.

"But I'm Pierre," she cried. "How could you?"

"Well, babe, it's lahke ya jerst ta old fer me. Ya even older than great-grandoor-er."

Pierre's heart was torn in two. She couldn't stand the treachery. "I'm going away. Don't try to find me as I don't know where I'm going."

Pierre got out her atlas. "Maybe I'll go to New York," she thought. "No one would think of looking for a model there."

In New York, she bought a little dog which she named Froggy. "You really are the dearest little fashion accessory," she giggled, as she sipped tea.

Pierre had many suitors who sent her roses. But all she longed for was a first edition of the seventh volume of Bill Wyman's history of the Rolling Stones.

She spent her days looking at the adverts in *Vogue* and having her hair cut. "I feel wonderfully fulfilled," she said to herself. "But something's missing."

"Hello," said the geriatric with the dancing eyes.

"I prefer OK!"

"Gimme shelter. Ah wahnt to have n' Aga n' babies. Be ma 11th wahfe."

And they both lived happily ever after for a couple of weeks.

The digested read ... digested

Jumping Jack Flash, it's just trash, trash, trash.

Asterix and the Actress

Albert Uderzo

"By Toutatis, is that you, Obelix?"

"Asterix, old friend, long time no see."

"It's been five years. We don't get out so much since poor old Goscinny died."

"So what are we up to this time?"

"The usual Doggybollox."

"I don't remember him."

"Get a life."

"Don't you mean Getafix?" asked the old druid.

"Go back to your magic potions," Asterix snapped. "Now, where was I? Ah yes! We're all sitting down to a village feast."

"It's all beginning to come back," interrupted Obelix, scratching his head quizzically. "Don't tell me I'm tucking into a whole wild boar and the Romans are terrified of us."

"Quite remarkable," said the little warrior hero. "Are you sure you haven't read this story already?"

"No."

"Oh well. So it's our birthday and our mummies have come to be with us."

"That means they'll be spending a few pages trying to find us both a wife."

"Ho ho ho," the two Gauls cackled in unison. "We're too young for that sort of responsibility. Ha ha. The old ones are the best."

"Ah. But what about our daddies?" asked Obelix.

"Sadly they've had to stay in Condatum to mind their Roman

souvenir shop. But they have sent us a super sword and helmet instead."

"I can add them to my collection."

"Yes, but old soak, Tremensdelirius, who sold them to our dads, happened to nick them off Pompey, the Roman general, and he wants them back. He's too frightened to send his legions in, so he gets the actress La Traviata to dress up as Panacea, Tragicomix's beautiful wife, in the hope that her feminine charms will get the armour back."

"Cor, do we get to kiss her?"

"No, but she does ask to see our swords."

"Oo-er," they both snorted.

"And then?" Obelix continued.

"The real Panacea and Tragicomix turn up, and there's lots of confusion but everything ends happily ever after with another feast."

"So, do I still get to carve menhirs and bash loads of Romans?"

"Do ursae shit in the sylvae?"

"I'm still not too clear what it was all about, though."

"Pure Economix," replied Uderzo.

The digested read ... digested

France's most successful resistance fighters creak into action to see off a few limp Romans with a few limp gags.

The Clematis Tree

Ann Widdecombe

Mark and Claire Wellings were goodish eggs, but the strain of looking after their disabled son, Jeremy, for 7 years had taken its toll. Their marriage was an empty, loveless shell.

"I've booked a holiday," said Mark.

"We can't leave Jeremy," Claire replied defiantly.

Mark knew his marriage was doomed.

Their daughter Pippa picked up a severe dose of gastroenteritis. "I hope Jeremy doesn't get it," Mark muttered to himself. "It could kill him." Jeremy spent the next two weeks in intensive care.

"That does for the holiday," said Mark over supper one evening. "By the way, did you know your sister Sally is planning to introduce a euthanasia bill into the Commons?" He wondered what the bill might mean for Jeremy and whether the press would discover his link to Sally.

Mark took himself off on a week's holiday to Estoril. He was awoken by some ice-cream dropping on his stomach. He looked up to see a girl with a hideous disfigurement.

"She seems very accepting of her condition," Mark said later to the girl's mother.

"I've taught her serenity," she said. "I'm a widow, incidentally."

They had dinner. Mark resisted the temptation of an affair, but still knew his marriage was doomed.

"I'm a shopaholic and I occasionally hit Jeremy," Claire confessed on his return.

"I'd better talk to the vicar, then," Mark concluded.

"I'm getting married to Ben," said Mark's sister Ruth. "His

first wife and two children were all killed in a car crash."

Mark's firm took on extra staff, including Ginny, a short-skirted Australian secretary. He resisted the temptation of an affair, but still knew his marriage was doomed.

Mark and Claire woke to find the press camped out on their doorstep. "They've found out about Jeremy," said Claire. Mark invoked the second person of the Trinity.

As Claire's father, Sam, lay in hospital after a severe stroke, Mark waved Pippa off on her school trip to France. "Have a safe journey," he shouted, as the coach departed.

Reports came in of a major accident, with several fatalities, on the M20. "I'm afraid Pippa was on the coach," said the headmaster. Mark and Claire waited anxiously for news.

"Actually, she was on the other coach after all," said the headmaster. "Pippa's fine."

Sam died of a heart attack and several months later the brake failed – or did aunt Isabel release it? – and Jeremy's wheelchair rolled into the river. Despite Mark's efforts to revive him, he drowned. "Could I have done more?" he anguished. "He looked so peaceful. But am I at peace?"

"I want a divorce," Mark said firmly.

"You can't," said Claire. "I'm pregnant."

Mark knew then he would stay in his doomed marriage of deepening unhappiness.

The digested read ... digested

The *Book of Job* rewritten for High Church, High Tory matrons from the shires.

The European Constitution

Digested live at the Guardian Hay Festival, May 2005

All Citizens shall have inalienable rights, Freedoms and principles to use capital Letters in an arbitrary manner, except where an individual Member State might find them awkward. In such cases, the Member State shall have the Competence to challenge the Competence of the Constitution in the European Court.

Citizens of the Union shall have the right to Move and Reside freely within the territory of the Member States, but only in so far as the Constitution is accorded such Competences in cases where the principle of Subsidiarity shall apply, the institutions of the Union shall apply the principle of Subsidiarity as laid down in the Protocol on the application of the principles of Subsidiarity and Proportionality.

The Union shall have Competence to define and implement a Common Foreign and Security policy, including the progressive framing of a Common Defence policy, except when such a Policy is too contentious for such a Common Defence policy to be framed.

The Union shall share Competence with the Member States where the Constitution confers on it a Competence which does not relate to the areas referred to in Article 1-13. Measures based on this Article shall not entail harmonisation of Member States' laws or regulations in cases where the Constitution excludes such Harmonisation. Duh.

The Union shall have exclusive Competence in matters of monetary policy for the Member States whose Currency is the euro; those Member States that insist on keeping their own currency shall be regarded as Off-message Member States and shall be treated accordingly.

The principle of voting by qualified majority, hereby defined as at least 55% of the members of the Council, comprising at least 15 of them and Representing Member States comprising at least 65% of the population of the Union, will be generally applied as the EU shall not be compromised by minority voices. However, the overarching Principle of Inaction shall be maintained by allowing any Member State a veto on foreign policy, defence and taxation. In any vote over what constitutes an area of veto in which a country has been outvoted, the Member State can take its case to the European Council, though it can still be outvoted there.

The Union shall have an institutional Framework which shall aim to promote its values, advance its Objectives and serve its interests and, where possible, those of its Citizens. This institutional framework comprises: the European Parliament, the European Council, the Council of Ministers, the European Commission, the Court of Justice of the European Union and the Council for the Processing of Expenses.

The President of the Commission shall lay down guidelines within which the Commission is to work and decide on the Internal organisation of the Commission. The Commission shall be an inclusive body and the President shall have Competence to appoint Homophobes and White-collar criminals. There will be 25 Commissioners from November, one for each Member State, though this figure shall be reduced to 18 in five years' time when the EU is more confident about ignoring the interests and Competences of smaller Member States.

The Constitution and law adopted by the Union institutions in exercising Competence conferred upon it by the Constitution shall have Primacy over the law of the Member States, though Member States shall be free to ratify their own internment Procedures for Asylum Seekers.

The Institutions shall, by appropriate means, give citizens and representative associations the opportunity to make known and publicly exchange their views in all areas of Union action. In areas of dispute, the Tripartite Social Summit for Growth and Employment shall contribute to social dialogue.

The Union does not endorse any particular Deity. This does not mean that such a Deity does or does not exist, only that if he or she does exist, then he or she has pan-European Competence.

A Member State which decides to withdraw from the EU shall notify the Council of its intention. The Union shall negotiate an Agreement with that State, setting out the arrangements for its withdrawal. If no satisfactory agreement can be reached, the Union shall have the Competence to declare war on that Member State.

The digested read ... digested

Incontinent incompetence from the continent

Bonus features

The Da Vinci Code

Dan Brown

Renowned curator Jacques Saunière shuddered. The first page of a Dan Brown potboiler was no place for any character. "Count yourself lucky," growled Silas the monk, as he chastised himself with his chalice. "I've got to hang around for another 400 pages of this badly written garbage."

The phone rang in Robert Langdon's hotel room. After his previous adventure with the Pope, nothing should have surprised him. But he was surprised. "I am surprised to be summoned to the Louvre in the dead of night," he said to himself.

Inspector Bezu Fache was as angry as his name suggested. "I don't like it when the renowned curator of the Louvre is found dead in the gallery at the dead of night in suspicious circumstances," he muttered. "So Monsieur Langdon. What do you make of Paris?"

"It is a very beautiful city, steeped in art and religion," replied Langdon earnestly. "And if I'm not very much mistaken, the pose Monsieur Saunière has adopted in death is highly symbolic."

"Not so fast," said a young woman, who identified herself as Sophie Neveu, an agent of the French cryptology department. "You have a phone call." She took him aside to the toilets. "Inspector Fache suspects you of the murder," she whispered. "You must run away with me, for I am Jacques Saunière's grand-daughter."

"Not before I have solved the riddle your grandfather left."

13-3-2-21-1-1-8-5

O Draconian devil!

Oh, Lame saint!

"Hmm, the numbers are the Fibonacci sequence," squeaked Sophie.

"And the words are an anagram for Leonardo da Vinci and the Mona Lisa."

They rushed to the world-famous painting. There they found another clue.

So dark the con of man

"It's another simple anagram," yelled Langdon. "Madonna of the Rocks." They rushed to the world-famous painting. There they found a key – another clue, before narrowly evading the combined forces of the Parisien gendarmerie.

"That was close," squealed Sophie.

"Thank goodness we have a long car ride to our next destination, as this will give me 20 pages to indulge in some bogus art history," said Langdon.

Sophie struggled to stay awake as Langdon droned on about the Leonardo, the feminine and Priory of Sion.

"Wasn't all this bollocks in *Holy Blood Holy Grail*?" she asked.

"Yes, but the Yanks will have forgotten all about it," Langdon replied.

They arrived outside the private Swiss bank. "You will need a combination as well as a key.

"It must be the Fibonacci sequence," Sophie yelled, as they collected the keystone to the Grail before narrowly evading the combined forces of the Parisien gendarmerie.

"We must take a long car journey to the home of the Sir Leigh Teabing, the eccentric crippled Grail expert who lives in France," said Langdon, "as this will give me time to indulge in some more bogus religious history. Did you know that Jesus married Mary

Magdalene and that they had kids. Mary is the Grail and your grandfather was the Grand Master of the Priory of Sion and you are a direct descendant of Jesus."

"And your sentence construction is pitiful," she laughed.

"Ah ha," said Sir Leigh, heaving his crippled leg across the room. "We have no time to lose if we are to unlock the riddle of the keystone. We must flee to England."

The private jet arrived at Biggin Hill, narrowly evading the combined forces of the Parisien Gendarmerie. Landon used the Atbash cipher and turned the keystone to S-O-F-I-A; it unlocked to reveal another riddle.

In London lies a knight a pope interred

They rushed to the Temple church. "This is a dead end," said Langdon, as Silas and Sir Leigh's manservant appeared. "He's been taken hostage," cried Sophie.

Langdon fretted over the riddle. He was in the wrong place. He rushed to Sir Isaac Newton's tomb in Westminster Abbey. There was Sir Leigh.

"I was the baddy all along," sneered Sir Leigh. "The Priory of Sion weren't going to release the secrets of the Grail so I persuaded Opus Dei to kill Saunière. Now I've killed Silas and the manservant and I want the cryptex."

Bezu Fache burst in and arrested Sir Leigh. "I apologise," he said. "You weren't the killer after all."

Langdon and Sophie took the train to Rosslyn in Scotland. "Will we find the grail here?" asked Sophie.

"No," said an old woman who turned out to be Sophie's grandmother.

Langdon shivered as he kissed the direct descendant of Jesus for the first time. Sophie smiled. Maybe she would see him again.

Langdon headed to Paris to start digging in the vaults under the Louvre. There he knelt before the bones of Mary Magdalene.

The digested read ... digested

Several million readers can all be wrong.

Harry Potter and the Half-Blood Prince

J.K. Rowling

The prime minister groaned as the minister of magic appeared. "There's trouble in the wizard world," said Cornelius Fudge. "We've got plenty of trouble in the Muggle world, too," the PM replied, happy to drop a knowing reference for the more adult readership.

Harry wasn't used to waiting until the third chapter to make an appearance. "Some years ago, I might have reacted a little petulantly," he muttered to himself, "but now I'm more grown up I'm happy to defer my gratification."

Dumbledore appeared at the door. "I've come to take you to the Weasleys," he said kindly. "And when you return to Hogwarts, you will be having some one-to-one tuition with me. You have so much back story to catch up on that you won't be ready for your final adventure unless you do a lot of cramming."

As Harry entered Hogwarts to start his sixth year, he was aware that the usual air of excitement was missing. Everything seemed rather the same, and even the thought of playing Quidditch left him feeling a little flat.

Even his relationships with Ron and Hermione felt stale. Sure the hormones were kicking in, and there was a lot of snogging, but it all felt laboured. Couldn't everyone see that Ron was only dating Lavender to annoy Hermione and that by the end of the book Ron and Hermione were bound to be a couple?

Harry tried to remain above such goings on. He was the Chosen One after all. "For the time being," he thought, "I will express my new found maturity by being more bad-tempered and swearing a bit." But, in time, even he couldn't resist the charms of Ginny Weasley.

A summons arrived from Dumbledore. At their previous meetings, Dumbledore had explained how Tom Riddle had become Lord Voldemort; now he wanted more. "You must persuade Professor Slughorn to share his memory with you."

"How am I going to do this?" Harry asked Hermione. "And why doesn't Dumbledore believe that Malfoy and Snape are up to no good?"

"Brilliant work," cried Dumbledore. "Now we know that Voldemort has split his soul into seven Horcruxes. We have destroyed two: only five to go before he can be defeated."

Dumbledore and Harry apparated to a cave in search of the third Horcrux, and returned to find Hogwarts under the shadow of the Dark Mark of the Death Eaters. A furious battle ensued and a central character lay dead, while Snape declared himself to be the Half-Blood Prince and disappeared with Malfoy into the night. The only message of hope was from someone who signed himself RAB.

"We have to split up, Ginny," said Harry grimly. "I can't put you in any more danger. A man's got to do what a man's got to do."

"Oh no he doesn't," Hermione and Ron chipped in. "We're coming with you."

The digested read ... digested

Back to the future.

Cell

Stephen King

Clayton Riddell was bouncing along Boylston Street in Boston when the event that came to be known as the PULSE took place. As is usual at the start of horror fiction, Clay was feeling good. Real good. He was on his way back to Maine to see if he could get back together with his wife, Sharon, and son, Johnny G.

A lady lifted a cell phone to her ear and sank her teeth into the neck of her friend. Blood spurted like a geyser. A man bit the head off a dog, a plane crashed on the next block and the streets ran red.

"Mustn't use the cell phone," Clay said to himself. He ran back to his hotel, dodging the crazies. He found another man — Tom — cowering in the corner and a 15-year old girl — Alice — being attacked by her mother. Clay picked up a metal spike and rammed it through the woman's carotid and left her twitching on the pavement.

"Have you noticed how they seem to go quiet and flock together at dusk?" said Clay, who didn't wonder why no one else in Boston appeared to have realised this. "We can leave the city by night."

The three travelled north, passing countless scenes of unspeakable violence involving mutilated corpses and severed limbs, which they were happy to speak about at length, till they arrived at Gaiten Academy. They were met by a boy called Jordan. "I've got a theory," said the annoyingly precocious Jordan. "The cell phone launched a computer program that erased the hard drive of every-one's brain."

"That sounds ridiculous enough for me to believe," Clay replied. "Let's torch the flock while they're resting at night."

The flames burnt bright and the stench of burning flesh hung in the air.

"We shouldn't have done that," said Tom.

"Why?"

"I can't tell you as it's just a device to artificially ratchet up the tension for 20 pages."

They all suffered the same nightmare in which the Rag-gedy Man appeared. "The crazies are psionic," muttered Clay. "They're invading our thoughts and telling us what to do."

"We are sparing you because you are insane," mouthed the Raggedy Man, with a logic that was hard to refute. "Go north."

The four followed the signs to KASHWAK= NO-FO. "It's a place where there's no phone masts," Clay pointed out help-fully, "We'll be safe. But first I've got to find my family."

Alice had a hideous accident and took 10 pages to die, but the others pressed on. "It's no good," said Tom. "Sharon is a crazy and Johnny G has been taken prisoner."

"I know," said Clay, "but I still must find him."

"And we'll go with you even though we know it's a trap because the Raggedy Man is making us," Tom answered.

"He's just a pseudopod," Jordan piped up. "There was a virus in the programme and the new crazies are behaving differently. Maybe everyone will eventually reboot to System Restore."

The bomb was ready. Clay dialled the number. The Raggedy Man melted as the Kashwak flock immolated. Tom and Jordan went north to Canada, but Clay still had to find Johnny G. There he was. Or was he? Should he call 911???

The digested read ... digested

A nuisance call.

Memories of My Melancholy Whores

Gabriel García Marquez

The year I turned 90, I wanted to give myself the gift of wild love with an adolescent virgin. I thought of Rosa Cabarcas, the brothel owner.

"You ask the impossible, my mad scholar," she said. But I implored her and she promised to ring back within the hour.

I'm ugly, shy and anachronistic, and I live alone in the house where my parents lived, scraping by on a meagre pension from my mediocre career as a journalist. And I have never been to bed with a woman without paying. In short, I am without merit or brilliance.

On the morning of my 90th birthday, I awoke, as always, at five in the morning. My only obligation was to write my signed column for Sunday's paper, for which, as usual, I would not be paid. I had my usual aches and pains - my asshole burned - but my heart lifted when Rosa rang to say I was in luck.

I gazed at the phosphorescent sweat on the naked body of the 14-year-old virgin asleep on the bed, and admired the brilliance of my language. "She was nervous," Rosa informed me, "so I gave her some Valerian."

She did not stir. "Let me call you Delgadina," I whispered, for like most solipsists I preferred to invent my own names. I may have slept myself and a tiger may have written on the bathroom mirror - we magical realists can never be too sure of anything - and when I left her snoring in the morning she was still as pure as the night before.

277

"You fool," spat Rosa. "She will be insulted you did not care enough about her to abuse her." But I did not care: I had detected the fragrance of Delgadina's soul and had realised that sex was the consolation we receive for the absence of love.

I had planned to tender my resignation at the paper, but I was so moved at being given a voucher to adopt a stray cat that shat and pissed at will, that I resolved to continue.

And my fame grew. Every evening I would go to Rosa's house and spend the night admiring the sleeping Delgadina - whose body was filling out agreeably - while reading out loud the great works of literature; and by day people would read out loud the tacky sentimentality of my columns.

Late into the year, Rosa interrupted my reveries. "A client has been murdered," she shouted. "Help me move him."

I returned night after night, but Rosa's house was locked up. I pined for Delgadina. I sensed my cat might lead me to her, but like my own writing, he led me up a cul-de-sac.

At last, Rosa returned. "Whore," I said. "You have sold Delgadina to secure your freedom."

"How wrong you are," she cried. "Others may consider you a sordid, delusional old man, but Delgadina loves you. She kept her distance because she wanted to save herself for you."

My heart soared. I was not a perv. I was a 91-year-old man with so much love to give and so much life to live. I will survive.

The digested read ... digested

100 pages of turpitude.

A Summer Crossing

Truman Capote

"You are a mystery, my dear," Lucy McNeil said, and her daughter Grady smiled indulgently. "Why, I guess I am a little perverse," she replied.

"Well I will worry about you," her mother continued. "Seventeen is very young to stay on your own in New York. But I shall bring you back the finest ball gown for your society debut."

"I can't think why Grady doesn't want to go to Europe with you," snapped Apple who, being eight years the older, was by far the more sensible of the McNeil sisters.

But Grady could not tell the truth. Be proud, she said to herself, and fly your pennant high above and in the wind.

A voice echoed in the hall. "Hello McNeil." It could only be Grady's friend, Peter Bell, and the pair giggled and sipped champagne as her parents prepared to depart. Lucy looked on kindly as Peter was from a well-to-do family.

"I wish that you could love me as I love you," Peter sighed. Poor Peter, Grady thought. How little he knows me. Perhaps one day I can tell him.

Grady strolled to the Broadway parking lot. She looked down at the young man. "Light me a cigarette," he growled.

Clyde Manzer was not the first lover she had ever known, but he was the first with whom she had been truly smitten. When they kissed, she could sense a raw, mumbling power.

"I love you," Grady mewed. Clyde said nothing. Since the war had ended, his life had been a disappointment. Was working in a parking lot the best he could expect? He knew the affair with

Grady McNeil was going nowhere. He was down-at-heel and had friends called Mink and Gump. Worst of all, he was Jewish.

"I don't care if you're Jewish," Grady cried. "Come back to my Fifth Avenue apartment and I'll bake you a cake."

Clyde buttoned his flies and switched on the ball game. "I love you so much," Grady pleaded as she lay naked on the bed. "Why can you not love me?" Ah, what the hell, thought Clyde, and they were married in secret that afternoon.

Grady languished alone in the New York heatwave. She knew why she was so reluctant to tell her family about the wedding, but why could Clyde not tell his? They were such a sweet Jewish family and she felt so welcome. And why did Clyde spend so little time with her? How lucky she was to still have Peter as a friend, because otherwise she would never go out at all.

The apartment had been empty for days and Clyde was getting curious. "I believe she's visiting her sister in the Hamptons," the valet said.

"Why Grady," said Apple. "There's this man at the door. He says he's your husband. Tell me it's not true."

"But it is," wailed Grady. "And I'm 16 weeks pregnant. Mother and father return next week. Whatever shall I do?"

"I'm taking you home," growled Clyde.

"Oh no you don't," said Peter.

The two men grappled in the back of the Buick as Grady drove over the Queensboro Bridge while inhaling deeply on a reefer.

"Damn it, you'll kill us all."

And not a moment too soon, thought the reader.

The digested read ... digested

Adolescent fumblings — on and off the page.

Blue Shoes and Happiness

Alexander McCall Smith

Mma Ramotswe sat out under the hot Botswanan sun drinking a cup of red bush tea. She picked up the paper and started chuckling at the new advice column, Aunty Emang. At her age there were some things you just knew. There were the difficult problems, such as why a wheel was round, and the trivial, such as where her husband, Mr JLB Matekoni, had left his toothbrush.

And it was in these very trivial problems that the only begetter of the No 1 Ladies' Detective Agency specialised. "Men are weak," Mma Ramotswe mused. Her assistant, Mma Makutsi, sensed another profound insight was imminent. "Mr JLB Matekoni's weakness is cake."

This was indeed interesting and worthy of another cup of tea. Mma Makutsi went to the kitchen where she encountered Mr JLB Maketoni."Sometimes a football team wins," he said. "And sometimes it loses."

This second piece of wisdom in as many minutes was interrupted by a shout. "There's a cobra in my office," cried Mma Ramotswe.

Just then Mr Whitson, one of Mr JLB Matekoni's customers, rushed in and grabbed the snake. "You're safe now," he said. "By the way, I wonder if you can help. All the local people near the game reserve are acting strangely."

It sounded like witchcraft to Mma Ramotswe, but she decided to say nothing as a distressed young woman, wearing an apron covered in food, entered the room. "I would guess that you are a cook," said Mma Ramotswe. "You are truly gifted with second sight," the girl answered. "I am at my wit's end. Mma Tsau is giving away free food to her husband and she thinks I am blackmailing her about it."

Mma Ramotswe drank her tea and smiled kindly. "Leave it to me." Mma Makutsi was very disturbed.

Her fiance, Phuti Radiphuti, had fallen silent when she had declared herself to be a feminist.

"You must cook him a meal to reassure him," Mma Ramotswe insisted. Mma Makutsi followed this excellent advice to the letter, but Phuti failed to arrive. "Oh what shall I do?" she cried. "You must go and talk to him," said Mma Ramotswe.

"Oh thank God, you're here," said Phuti. "I was unexpectedly called away and I was worried you might think I did not want to marry you anymore." Mma Ramotswe sighed with the release of such unbearable tension.

A nurse darted into the office. "There's something strange about the Ugandan doctor," she said. "He's giving the wrong blood pressure pills."

Mma Ramotswe noted down the details before accompanying Mma Makutsi to buy some new shoes. "They look a little small."

Mr Polopetsi had grown concerned that Mma Ramotswe had made no attempt to solve any of her cases, so he drove to Mr Whitson's game reserve.

"The locals were superstitious about the hornbill," he said later.

"Sadly, it's now a late hornbill as you put it in a box," Mma Ramotswe observed tartly. "And by the way, Aunty Emang was responsible for Mma Tsau's and the Ugandan doctor's troubles."

Mma Makutsi grinned. Mma Ramotswe had saved the day again. "Time for tea," said Mma Ramotswe.

The digested read ... digested

Much ado about nothing.

False Impression

Jeffrey Archer

9/10 — Lady Victoria Wentworth never heard the young woman break into her stately home. Minutes later she lay dead with her throat slit and her ear removed.

9/11 — Today Fenston would get his hands on the Van Gogh. Few suspected that behind his facade as a respected banker lay one of Ceausescu's most loyal cronies who had amassed a fabulous horde of impressionist art by getting rich collectors to borrow money at ridiculous rates of interest and then killing them.

Anna Petrescu, the world's most fragrant expert on impressionist paintings, entered the North Tower and took the elevator for her meeting with her boss.

"The Wentworth Van Gogh should be sold to Nakamura," she said. "That way, she can pay her debts and keep her home."

"You're fired," Fenston yelled and left. Anna went to her office and the walls exploded around her. She was the last person to leave the tower alive.

"Hmm," she thought. "Everyone will assume I'm dead. Maybe I can use that to my advantage and save the Wentworth Van Gogh."

9/12 — Anna ran the last six miles to the Canadian border and flew to London.

"Aha," said Fenston. "She's gone to London via Canada."

He picked up the phone and called Krantz, his personal 4ft 11in female Romanian assassin.

Jack observed Anna and Fenston from afar. "Maybe if I repeat the fact that Anna has gone to London via Canada it will make it seem less ridiculous," he told his CIA minder.

9/13 — Anna arrived in London, hijacked the Van Gogh, had a secret meeting with Victoria's sister, Lady Arabella and left for Bucharest with a parcel.

"She's leaving for Bucharest," said Krantz, getting on the same plane.

"She's leaving for Bucharest," said Jack, getting on the same plane.

9/14 — Anna met with her old art teacher and asked him a special favour. "Because of all the charitable works you have done, I cannot refuse," he said.

"She's leaving for Tokyo," said Krantz, getting on the same plane.

"She's leaving for Tokyo," said Jack, getting on the same plane.

9/15 — "You are a remarkable woman, Miss Petrescu," bowed Nakamura. "I will do as you say".

Krantz hung on to the bumper of Nakamura's car for 40 miles before holding up the driver. She ripped open the parcel. It was the wrong painting.

"She's going back to Bucharest," said Krantz, getting on the same plane.

"She's going back to Bucharest," said Jack, getting on the same plane.

9/16 — Anna had another secret meeting with her art teacher before leaving for London. The taxi driver shot Krantz in the shoulder. "That's for all those who died under Ceausescu," he muttered.

9/18 — Fenston unwrapped the Van Gogh. "It's a fake," sneered the insurers.

9/19 — Jack phoned his minder. "Krantz escaped from 17 guards at the hospital."

9/20 — Arabella, Anna and Nakamura celebrated the sale of the Van Gogh. "Not so fast," laughed Krantz. Arabella, who had a touch of Margaret Thatcher's steel, blasted her with a shotgun.

Jack rushed in. "I've just realised that Fenston is wearing one of Victoria's earrings, so everything's sorted." He gazed into Anna's millpond eyes. "Come back to Grantchester with me."

The digested read ... digested

Crook tries to make money out of 9/11. Just like his characters.

Acknowledgments

Sometimes it feels as if the Digested Read writes itself. This is a delusion. So, many thanks are due to Lisa Darnell, Ben Seigle, Ruth Petrie, Michael Hann, Toby Manhire, Matt Keating, Felicity Lawrence, Leo Hickman, Ian Katz, Kath Viner, Will Woodward, Claire Phipps, Genevieve Carden, Paul Howlett, Esther Addley, Paul Macinnes, Roger Rapoport and Richard Harris.